The Black K
Brothers

Transcribed by Steve Gorenberg

Cherry Lane Music Company
Director of Publications/Project Editor: Mark Phillips

ISBN 978-1-60378-324-8

Visit our website at www.cherrylaneprint.com

EVERLASTING LIGHT

Words and Music by
Dan Auerbach and Patrick Carney

Intro
Moderately slow Rock ♩ = 88

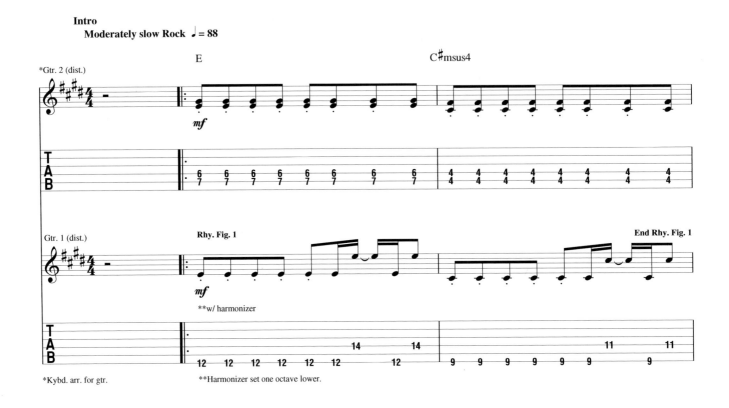

*Kybd. arr. for gtr.   **Harmonizer set one octave lower.

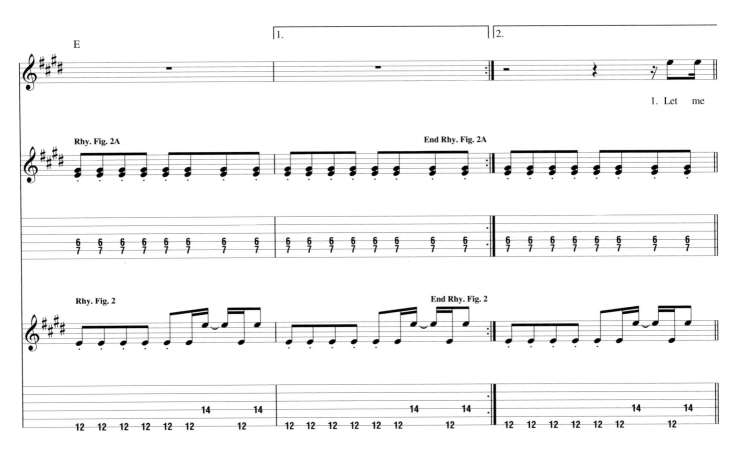

4

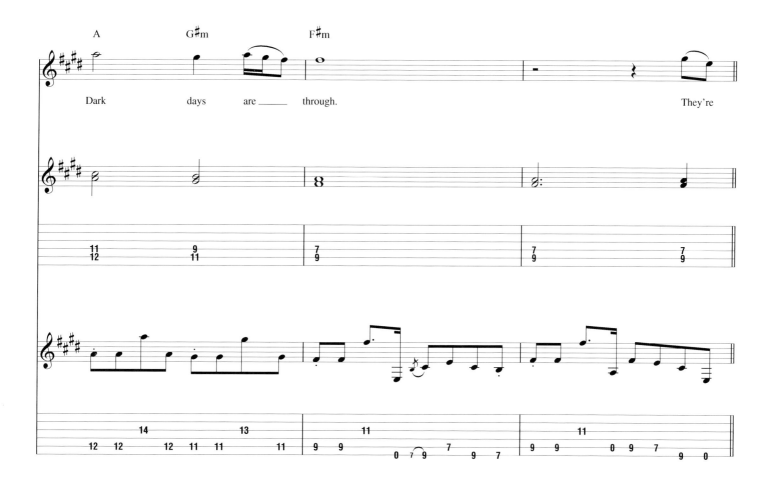

A   G#m   F#m

Dark   days   are _____ through.   They're

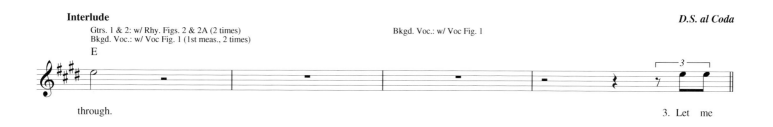

Interlude
Gtrs. 1 & 2: w/ Rhy. Figs. 2 & 2A (2 times)   Bkgd. Voc.: w/ Voc Fig. 1
Bkgd. Voc.: w/ Voc Fig. 1 (1st meas., 2 times)   *D.S. al Coda*

E

through.   3. Let   me

$\oplus$ **Coda**

Gtr. 1: w/ Rhy. Fig. 2   **Outro**
Bkgd. Voc.: w/ Voc Fig. 1 (1st meas., 2 times)   Gtr. 1: w/ Rhy. Fig. 1
                                              Bkgd. Voc.: w/ Voc Fig. 1 (1st meas., till end)

E   E

                           Yeah. __   Let   me   be   your   ev - er - last - ing   light. __

Gtr. 2

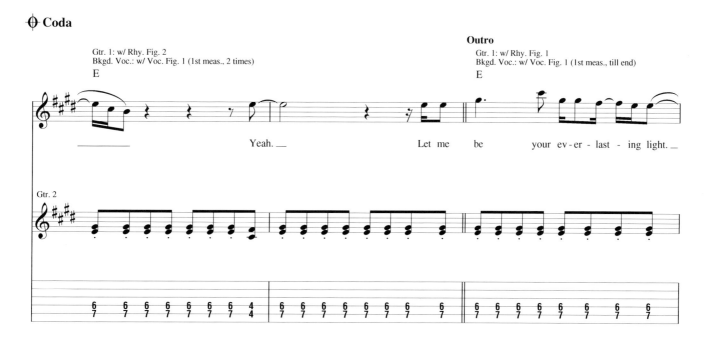

Let me be your ev - er - last - ing light, _____

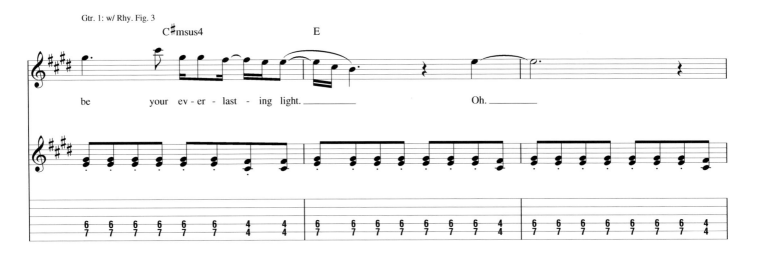

be your ev - er - last - ing light. _____ Oh. _____

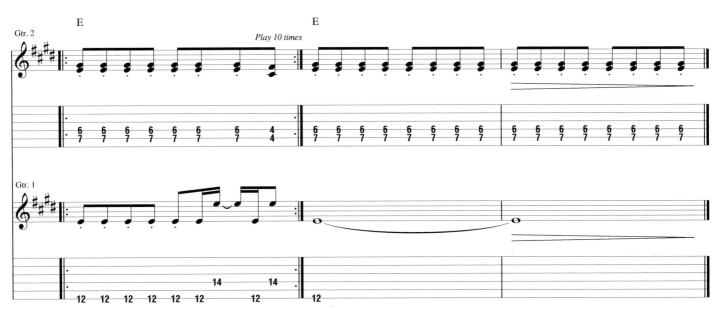

NEXT GIRL

Words and Music by
Dan Auerbach and Patrick Carney

Verse

Gtr. 1: w/ Riff A (2 times)

N.C.

a beau - ti - ful face ___ and a, and a wick - ed way, and I'm

pay - ing for her beau - ti - ful face ev - 'ry day.

All that work ___ o - ver, o - ver so much time; ___ if I,

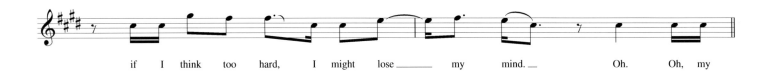

if I think too hard, I might lose ___ my mind. ___ Oh. Oh, my

Chorus

Gtr. 2: w/ Riff B (2 times)

N.C.

next girl, ___ yeah, will be noth - ing like my ex girl. ___

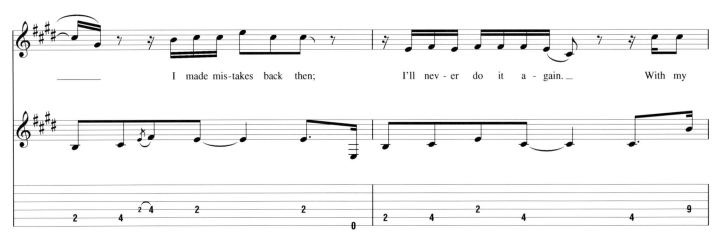

___ I made mis-takes back then; I'll nev - er do it a - gain. ___ With my

10

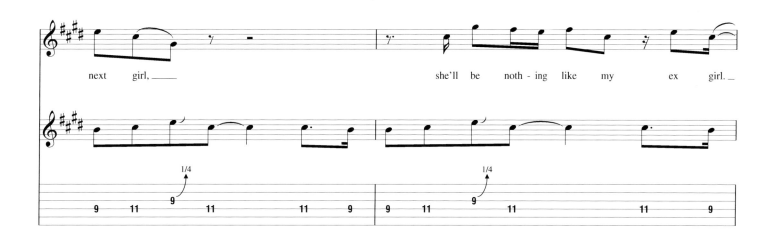

next girl, _____ she'll be noth-ing like my ex girl. _____

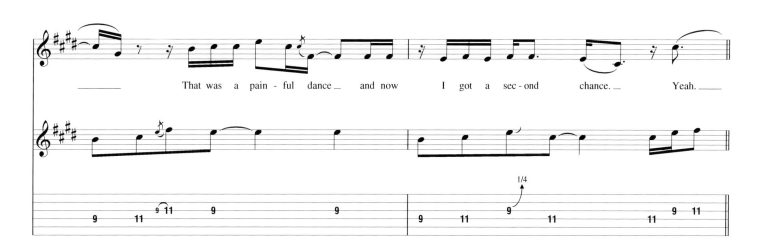

_____ That was a pain-ful dance _____ and now I got a sec-ond chance. _____ Yeah. _____

Interlude
N.C.

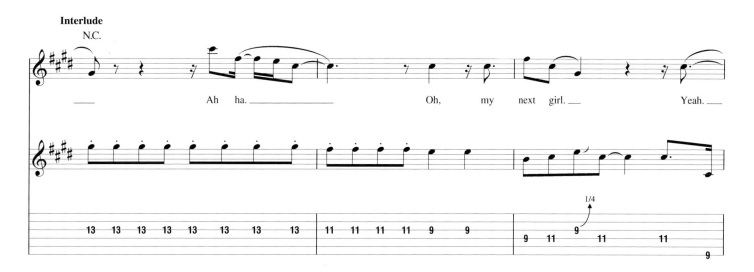

_____ Ah ha. _____ Oh, my next girl. _____ Yeah. _____

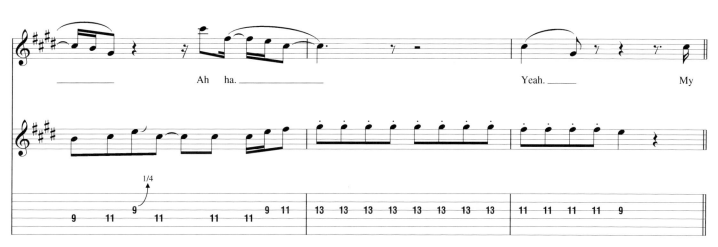

_____ Ah ha. _____ Yeah. _____ My

Gtr. 1: w/ Riff A (2 1/2 times)

N.C.

next   girl.

Gtr. 2

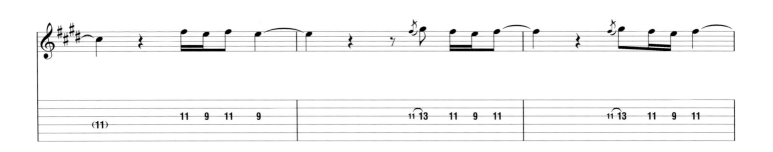

Gtr. 2

Gtr. 1

TIGHTEN UP

Words and Music by
Dan Auerbach and Patrick Carney

Some - one said __ true love __ was dead __ and I'm __ bound to fall, _____ bound
times like these __ I need __ re - lief. Please show me how, _____ oh, show

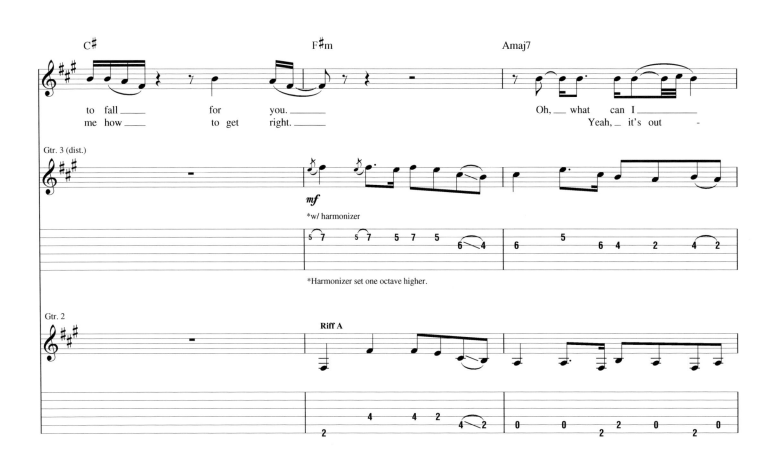

to fall ____ for you. ____ Oh, __ what can I
me how __ to get right. ____ Yeah, _ it's out -

Gtr. 3 (dist.)

mf

*w/ harmonizer

*Harmonizer set one octave higher.

Gtr. 2

Riff A

do? _ Yeah. _
ta sight.

Verse
Gtr. 1: w/ Rhy. Fig. 1 (2 times)

2. Take my __ badge, __ but my
4. When I was young __ and mov -

End Riff A

Gtrs. 2 & 3 tacet

Amaj7   Bm   C#

heart re - mains ___ lov - in' you, ___ ba - by child. ___
- ing fast, noth - ing slowed me down, ___ oh, slowed me down. ___

Gtr. 2: w/ Riff A

F#m   Amaj7   Bm

Tight - en ___ up ___ on ___ your reigns; you're run - nin' wild, ___ run -
Now I let ___ the oth - ers pass. ___ I've come a - round, ___ oh, come

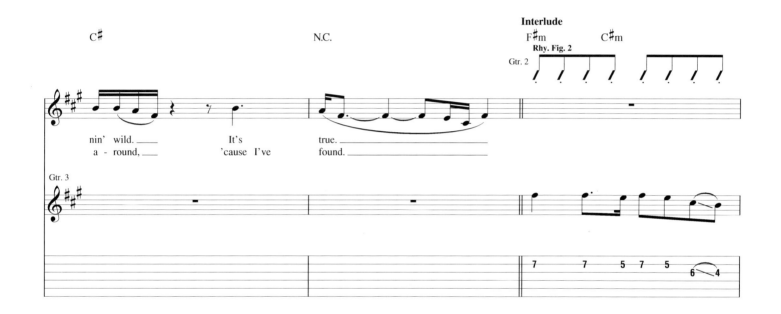

C#   N.C.   **Interlude**
F#m   C#m
Rhy. Fig. 2
Gtr. 2

nin' wild. ___ It's true. ___
a - round, ___ 'cause I've found. ___

Gtr. 3

```
7      7   5 7  5      6  4
```

F#m   C#m   F#m   C#m   A   B   **End Rhy. Fig. 2**

```
5 7    7   5 7 5  6  4    5 7    7   5 7 5  6  4    4 6   6   4 6 2 2      1/4
                                                                  4  2
```

Gtr. 2: w/ Rhy. Fig. 2

F#m   C#m   F#m   C#m   F#m   C#m

```
7   7   5 7 5  6  4    7   7   5 7 5  6  4    7   7   5 7   5   7 5
```

HOWLIN' FOR YOU

Words and Music by
Dan Auerbach and Patrick Carney

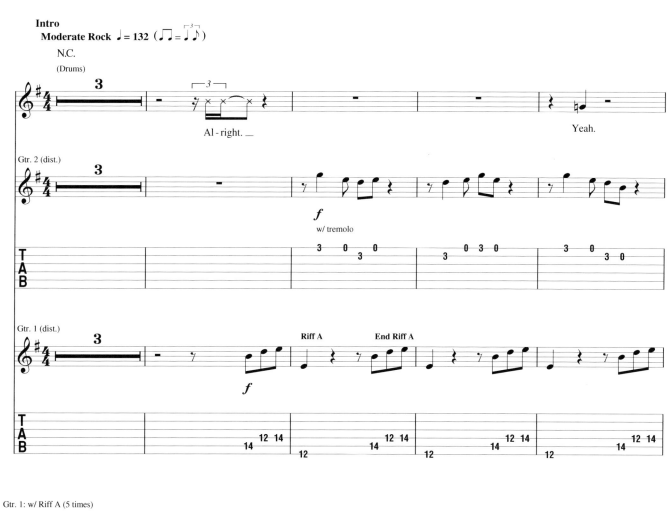

*Substitute quarter rest on beat 4 when Riff B1 is recalled.

Interlude

Gtr. 1: w/ Riff A (4 times)

N.C.

Gtr. 2

Verse

Gtr. 1: w/ Riff A (5 times)
Gtr. 2 tacet

N.C.

3. Mock - ing - bird,   can't you see?   The lit - tle   girl's   got a,

Gtrs. 1 & 2: w/ Riffs B & B1

a hold on me like glue.   Ba - by, I'm howl - in' for

Gtr. 1: w/ Riff A (4 times)

you.   Yeah.

Gtr. 2

Verse

Gtr. 1: w/ Riff A (5 times)
Gtr. 2 tacet

N.C.

4. Throw the ball   to the stick.   Swing and miss   in the

Gtrs. 1 & 2: w/ Riffs B & B1

catch - er's mitt: strike two.   Ba - by I'm howl - in' for

20

✛ Coda

Guitar Solo

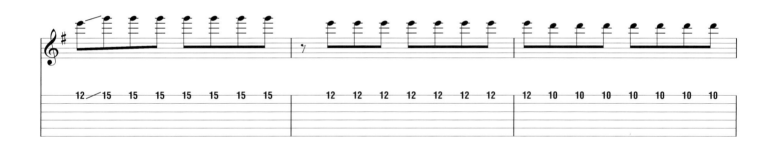

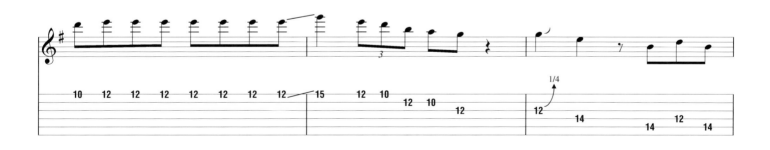

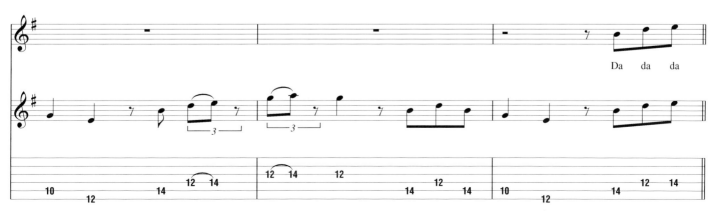

Chorus

Gtr. 1: w/ Riff C (2 times)
Gtr. 2: w/ Riff C1 (1 3/4 times)

N.C.

da   da,   da   da   da   da   da.   Da   da   da   da   da,   da   da   da   da   da.   Da   da   da

da   da,   da   da   da   da   da.   Da   da   da   da   da,   da   da   da

Guitar Solo

Gtr. 1: w/ Riff A (5 times)

N.C.

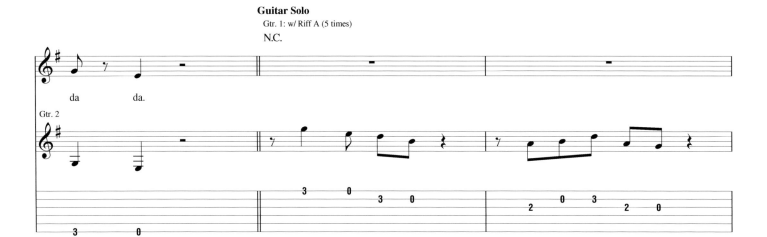

da   da.

Gtr. 2

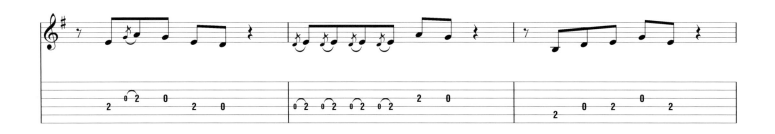

Gtr. 2

Gtr. 1

22

SHE'S LONG GONE

Words and Music by
Dan Auerbach and Patrick Carney

Intro
Moderately slow Rock ♩ = 77

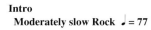

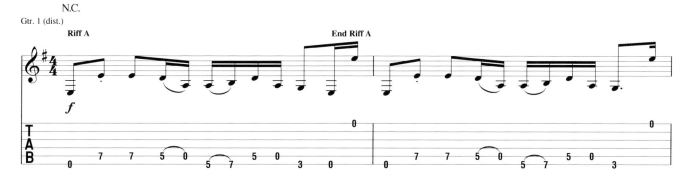

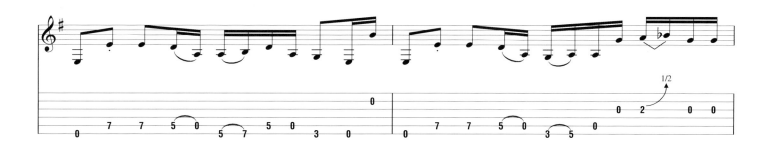

Gtr. 1: w/ Riff A (4 times)

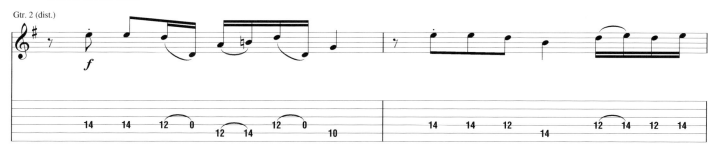

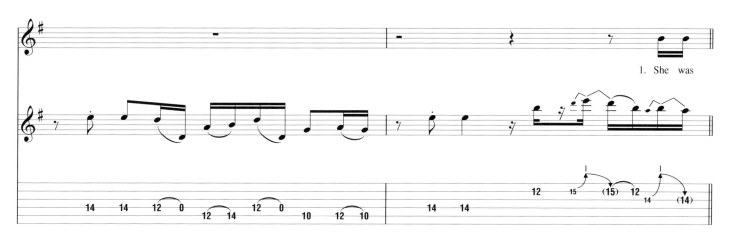

1. She was

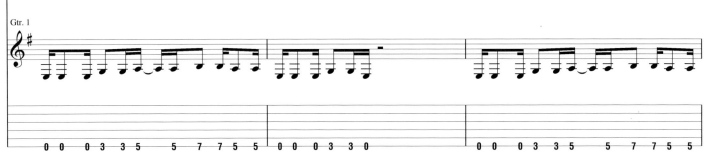

gone _____ like Mo - ses through the corn. _____ A - rock on. ___

Outro/Guitar Solo

Gtr. 1: w/ Riff A (15 times)

N.C.

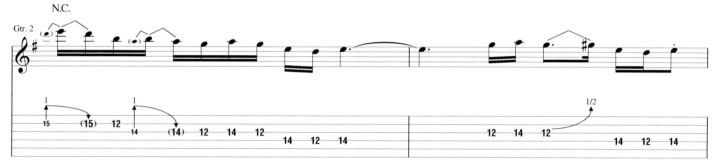

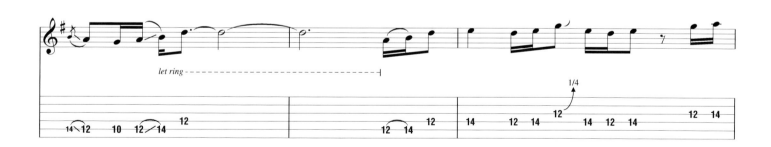

let ring -

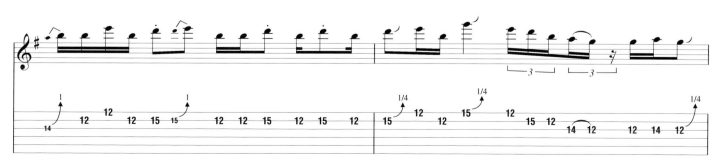

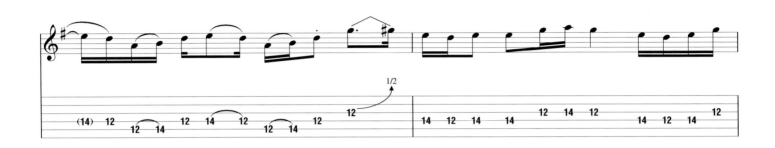

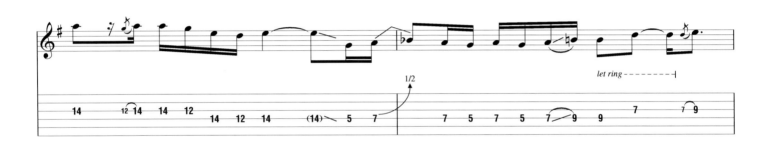

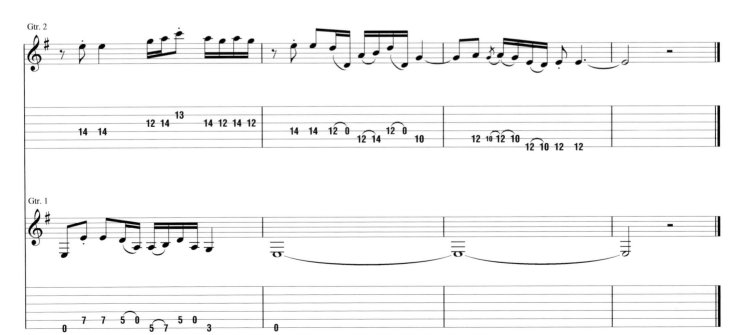

BLACK MUD

Words and Music by
Dan Auerbach and Patrick Carney

A

Moderately slow Rock ♩ = 74

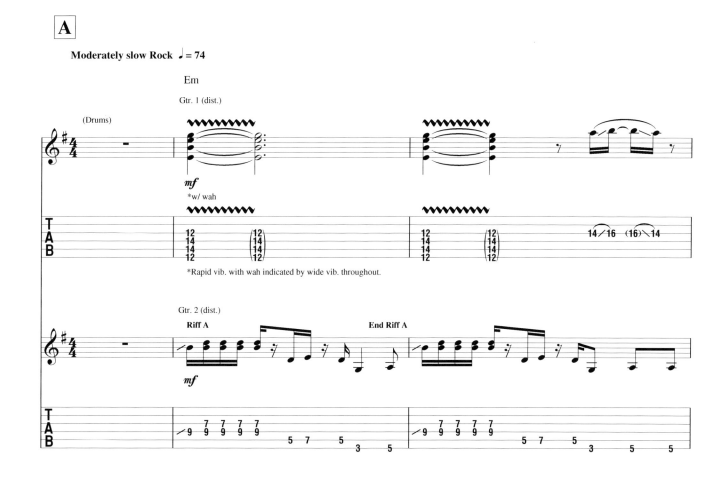

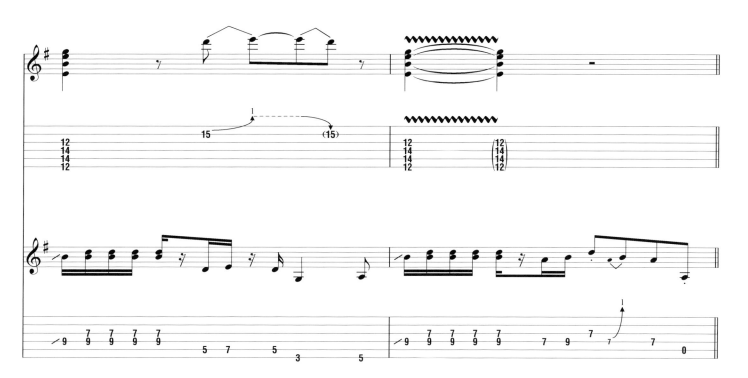

THE ONLY ONE

Words and Music by
Dan Auerbach and Patrick Carney

Intro
Moderate Rock ♩ = 105

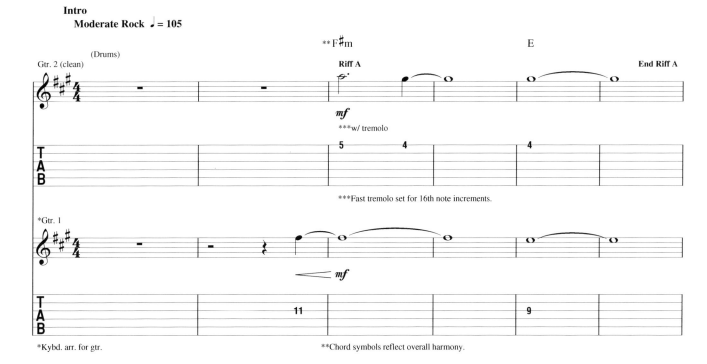

*Kybd. arr. for gtr.   **Chord symbols reflect overall harmony.

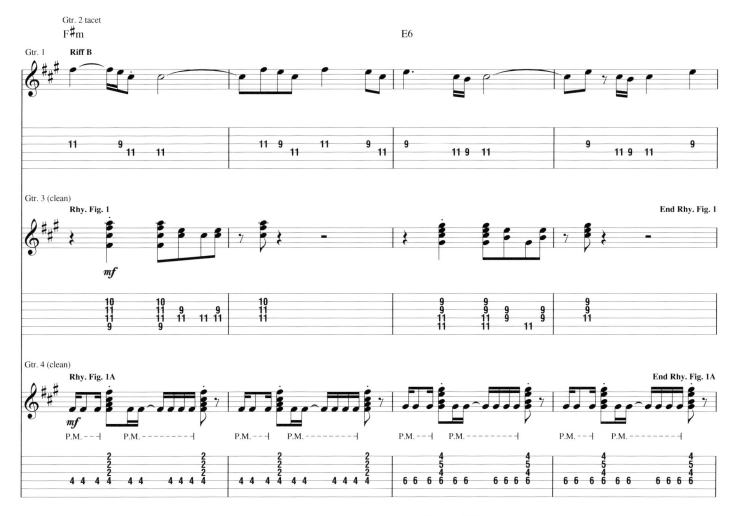

E

_____ when you're a — round. _____
_____ when I get near. _____

You're _ the

Chorus

Gtr. 2: w/ Riff A (5 times)

F#m

E6

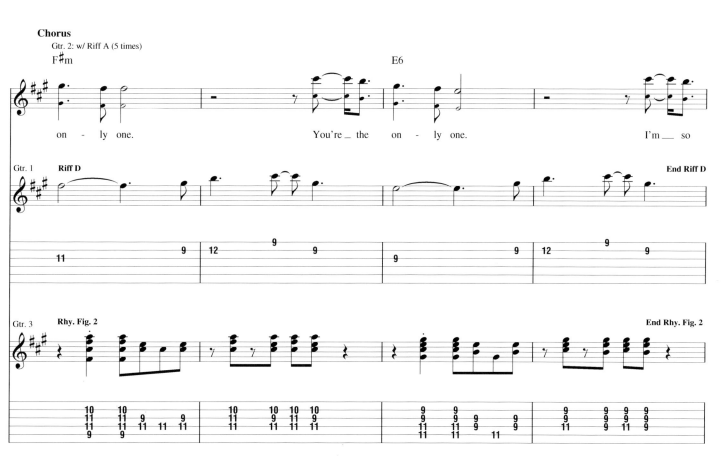

on — ly one.

You're _ the on — ly one.

I'm _ so

Gtr. 1 · Riff D · End Riff D

Gtr. 3 · Rhy. Fig. 2 · End Rhy. Fig. 2

1st time, Gtr. 1: w/ Riff D (4 times)
2nd time, Gtr. 1: w/ Riff D (3 3/4 times)
1st time, Gtr. 3: w/ Rhy. Fig. 2 (4 times)
2nd time, Gtr. 3: w/ Rhy. Fig. 2 (3 3/4 times)

F#m

E6

wrapped up in a daze, hop — ing this is just a

F#m

faze. But _____ when all is said and done, I _ know

E6

F#m

you are still the one. You're _ the on — ly one.

You're __ the on - ly one.   Cu - pid's

To Coda ⊕

bow, it stung, _____   now you're the on - ly one. _____

Interlude
Gtr. 1: w/ Riff B
Gtrs. 3 & 4: w/ Rhy. Figs. 1 & 1A (2 times)

D.S. al Coda

⊕ **Coda**

Interlude

Ah __ ha,

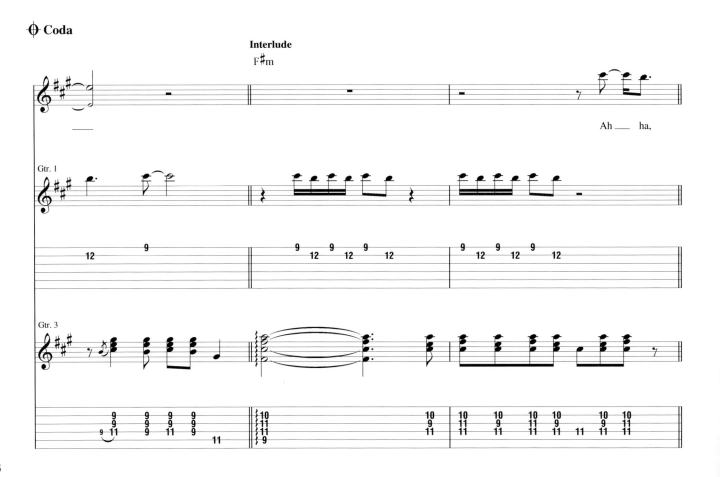

TOO AFRAID TO LOVE YOU

Words and Music by
Dan Auerbach and Patrick Carney

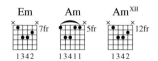

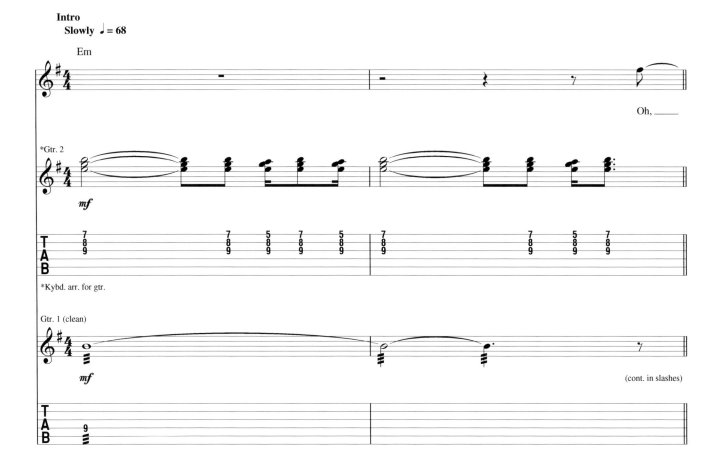

Gtr. 1: w/ Rhy. Fig. 1

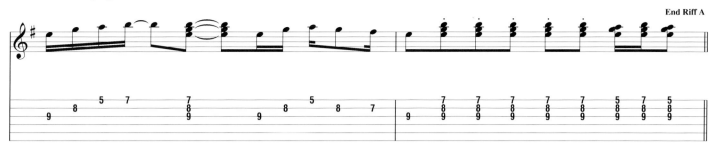

Verse

Gtr. 1: w/ Rhy. Fig. 1

Em

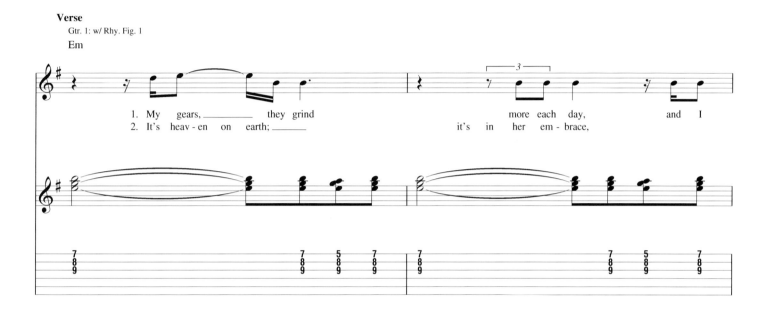

1. My gears, _____ they grind _____ more each day, _____ and I
2. It's heav-en on earth; _____ it's in her em - brace,

2nd time, Gtr. 1: w/ Rhy. Fig. 2

Am   *Am7/G   Em

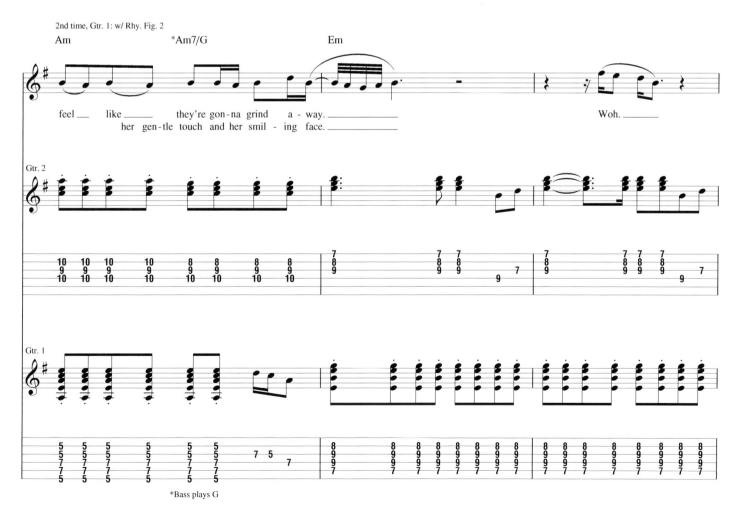

feel __ like _____ they're gon-na grind a - way._____   Woh._____
her gen-tle touch and her smil - ing face._____

Gtr. 2

Gtr. 1

*Bass plays G

Bridge

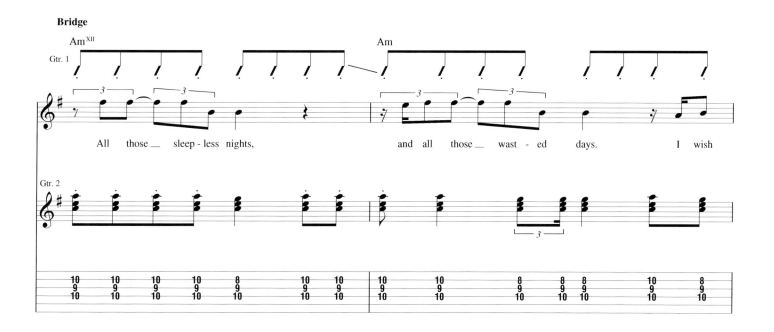

All those sleep-less nights, and all those wast - ed days. I wish

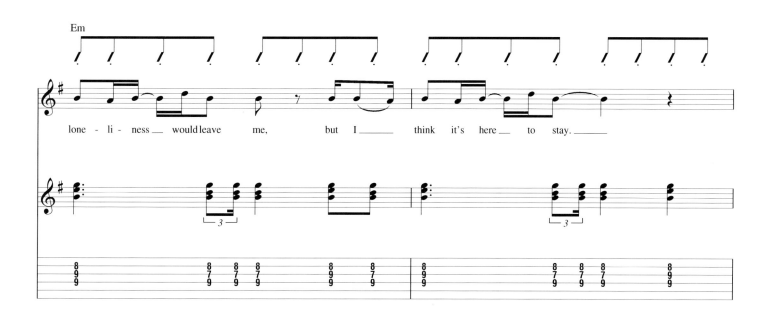

lone - li - ness would leave me, but I think it's here to stay.

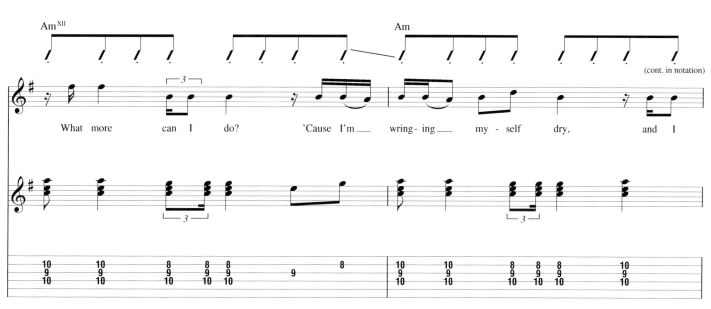

What more can I do? 'Cause I'm wring - ing my - self dry, and I

(cont. in notation)

41

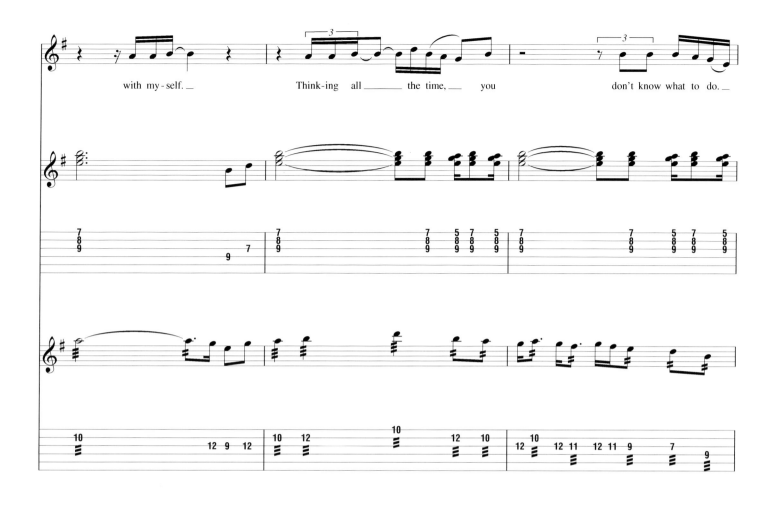

with my-self. ___ Think-ing all ___ the time, ___ you don't know what to do. ___

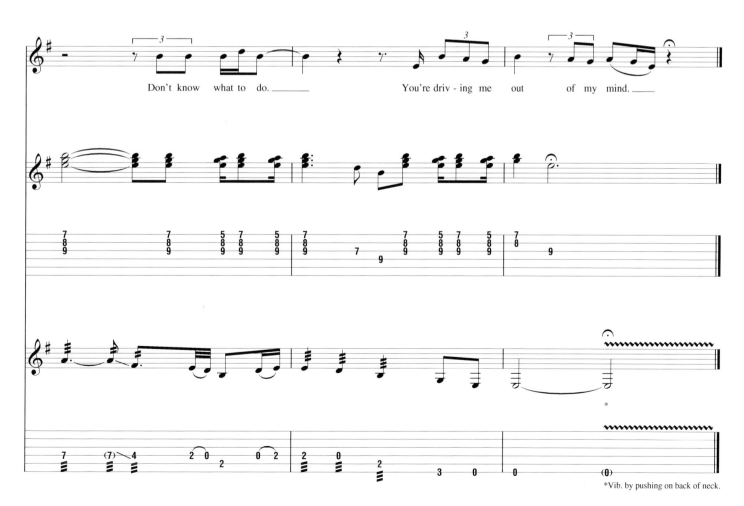

Don't know what to do. ___ You're driv-ing me out of my mind. ___

*Vib. by pushing on back of neck.

TEN CENT PISTOL

Words and Music by
Dan Auerbach and Patrick Carney

Intro
Moderate Rock ♩ = 104

*Fret low G (6th string) w/ thumb throughout.

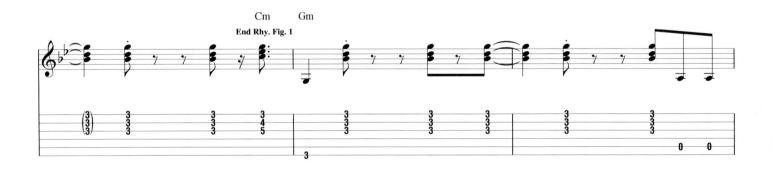

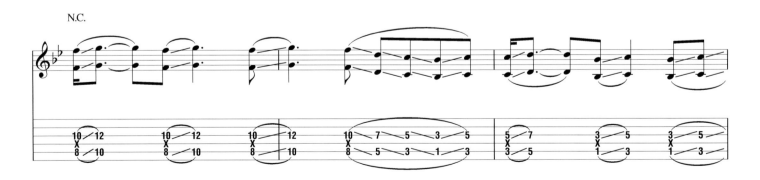

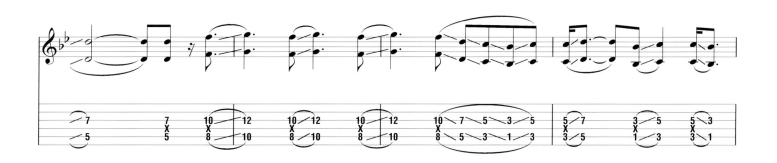

Gtr. 1: w/ Rhy. Fig. 1 (2 times)

1. Well, he ____

Verse

ran a - round ____ late at night, ____ hold - ing hands ____

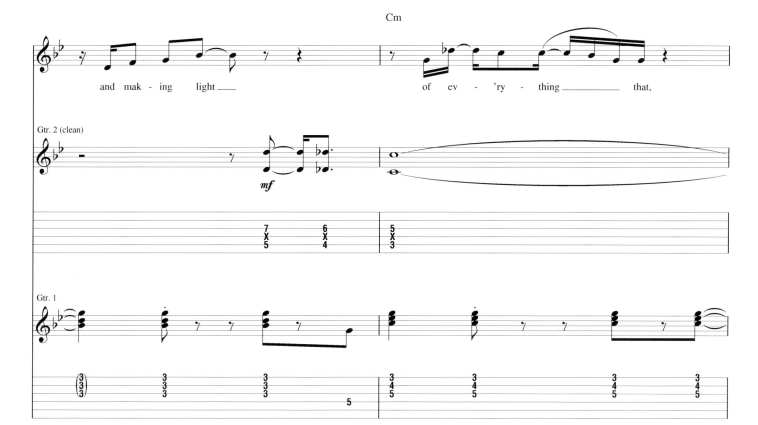

and mak - ing light ____ of ev - 'ry - thing ____ that,

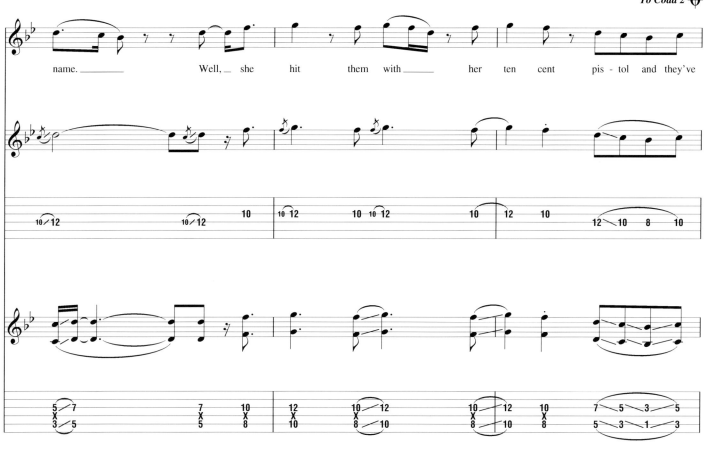

name._____ Well,_ she hit them with _____ her ten cent pis - tol and they've

Interlude

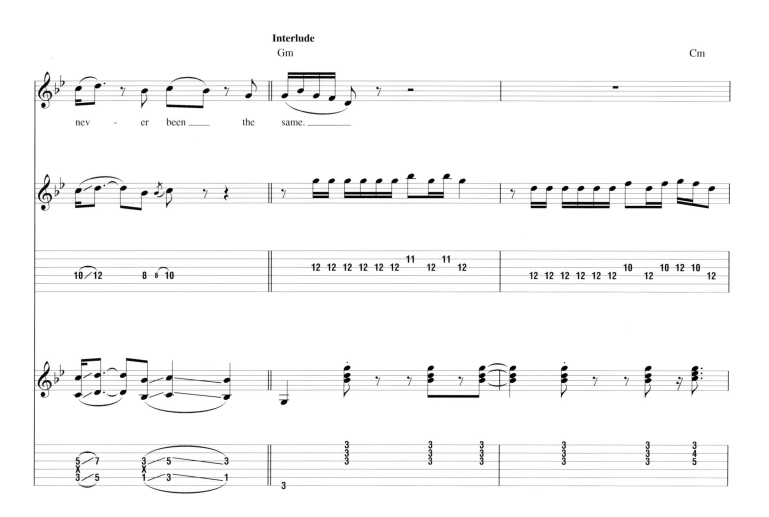

nev - er been _____ the same. _____

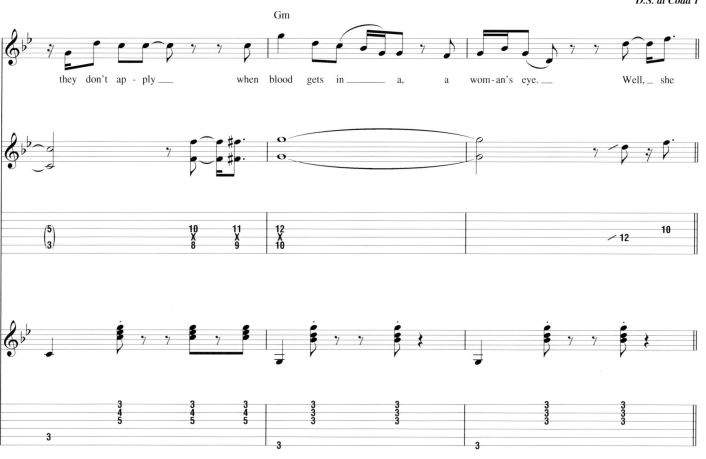

Gm

they don't ap - ply ____ when blood gets in ____ a, a wom-an's eye. ____ Well, __ she

⊕ Coda 1

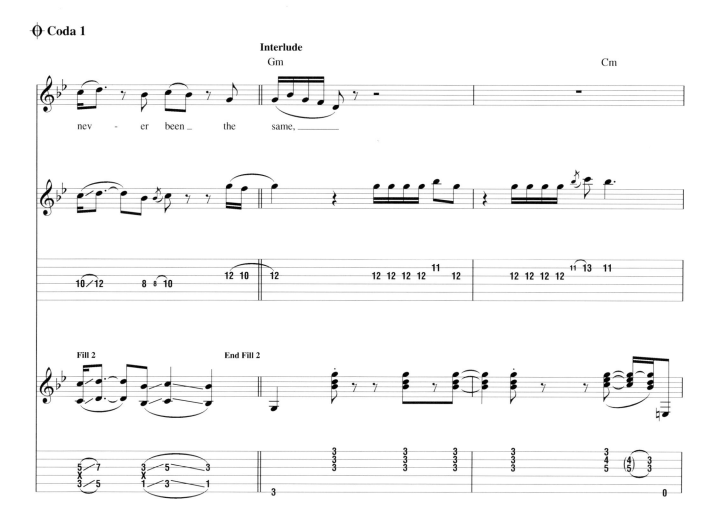

Interlude

Gm   Cm

nev - er been __ the same, ____

Fill 2   End Fill 2

*w/ harmonizer set one octave higher

Cm

*w/ harmonizer set one octave higher

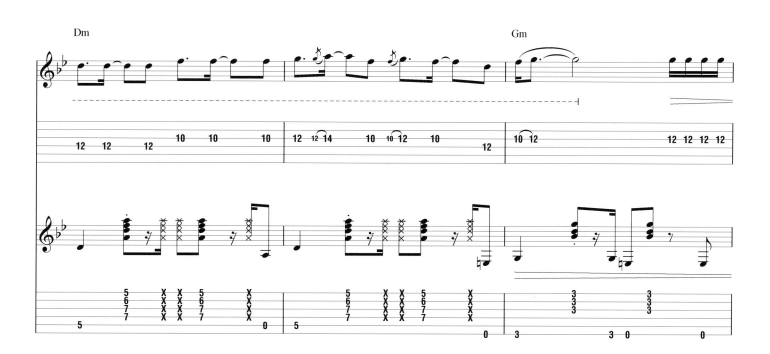

Dm

Gm

Verse

3. Stars did __ fall; thun-der rolled. Bugs __ crawled back

in their __ holes. __ The cou - ple screamed __ but it was far too late;

D.S. al Coda 2

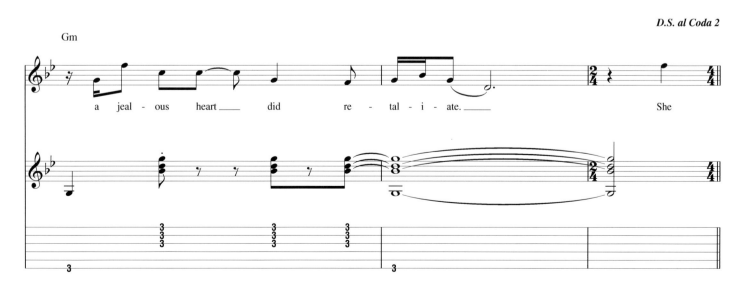

a jeal - ous heart __ did re - tal - i - ate. __ She

⊕ Coda 2

Outro

Gtr. 1: w/ Fill 2

Gtr. 1: w/ Rhy. Fig. 1 (5 times)

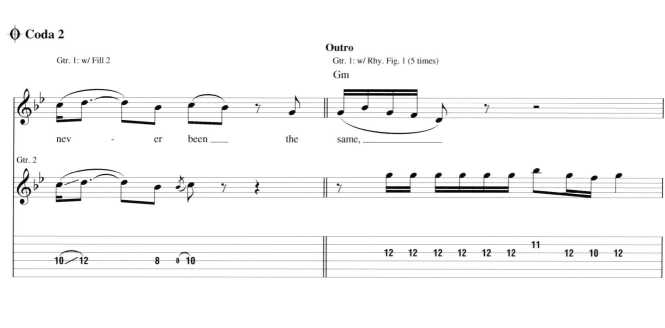

nev - er been ___ the same, _____

Gtr. 2

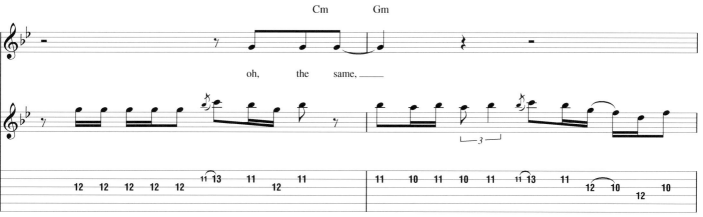

oh, the same, ___

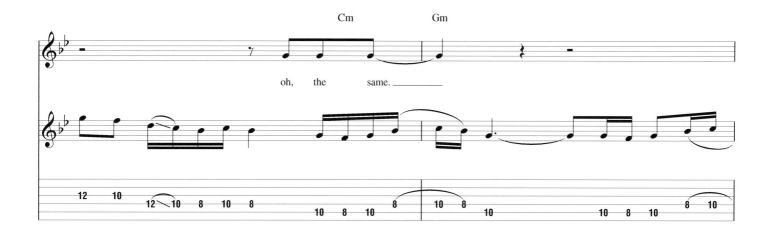

oh, the same. _____

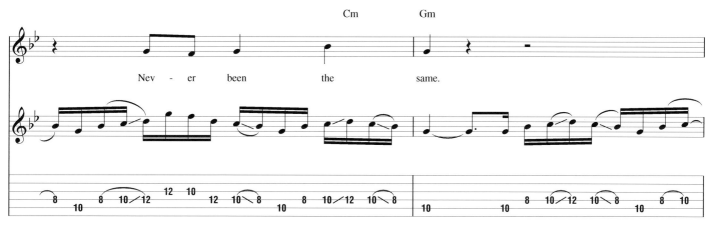

Nev - er been the same.

SINISTER KID

Words and Music by
Dan Auerbach and Patrick Carney

Intro
Moderately slow Rock ♩ = 68

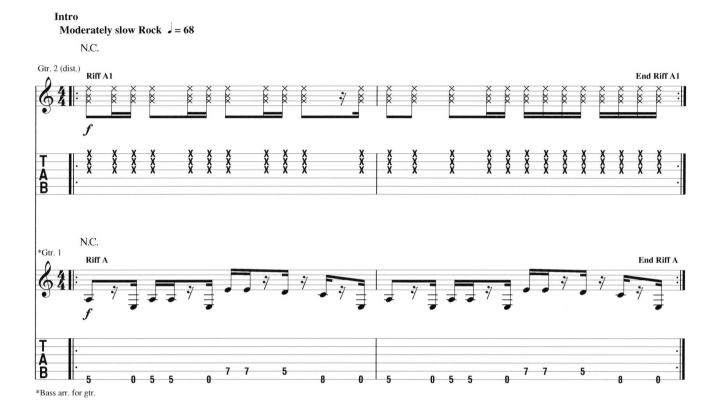

*Bass arr. for gtr.

Gtr. 1: w/ Riff A (2 times)
**Gtr. 2: w/ Riff A1 (till end)

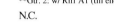

**Gtr. 2 continues muted strumming pattern w/ sporadic rhythmic variations throughout.

Verse

Lyrics: 1. Well, the crooks are out ___ and the streets are ___ grey.

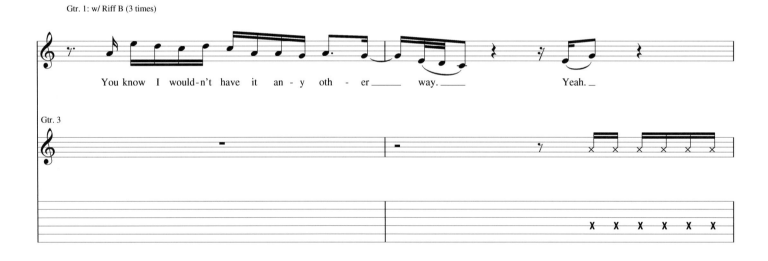

Gtr. 1: w/ Riff B (3 times)

Lyrics: You know I would-n't have it an-y oth-er ___ way. ___ Yeah. ___

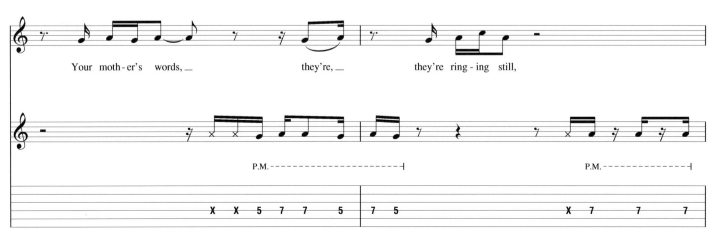

Lyrics: Your moth-er's words, ___ they're, ___ they're ring-ing still,

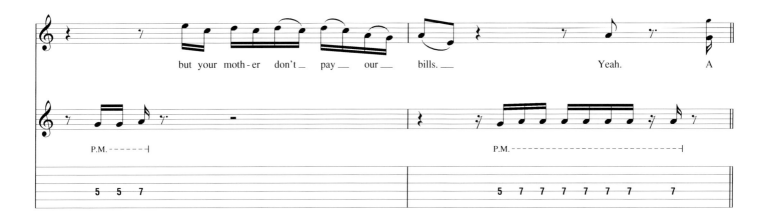

but your moth-er don't __ pay __ our __ bills. __ Yeah. A

Chorus
Gtr. 1: w/ Riff A (4 times)
N.C.

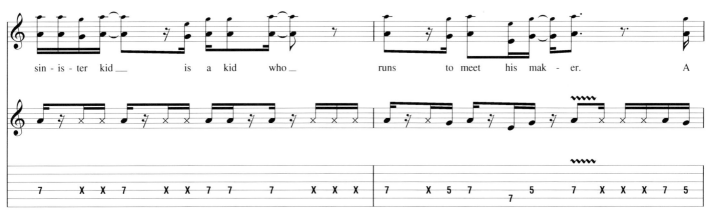

sin - is - ter kid __ is a kid who __ runs to meet his mak - er. A

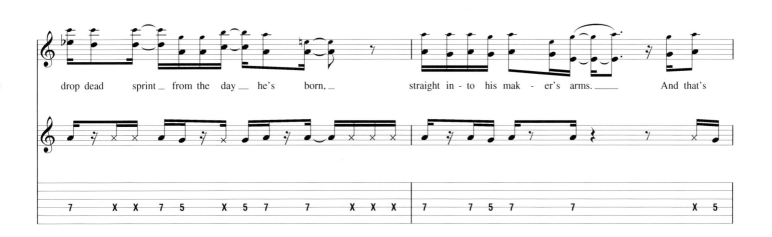

drop dead sprint __ from the day __ he's born, __ straight in - to his mak - er's arms. ____ And that's

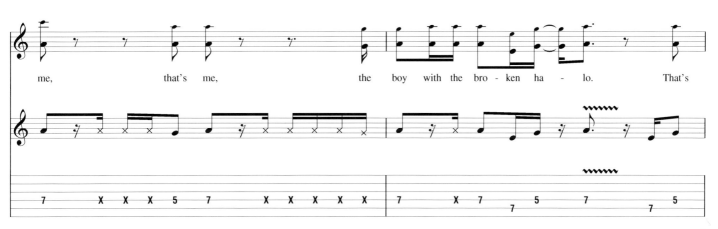

me, that's me, the boy with the bro - ken ha - lo. That's

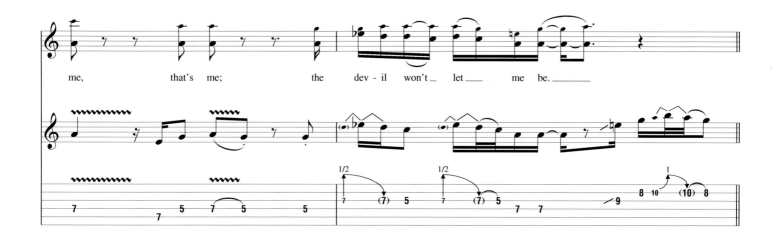

me, that's me; the dev-il won't___ let___ me be._____

Verse

Gtr. 1: w/ Riff B (4 times)

N.C.

2. I got a tor-tured mind,_____ and my blade is sharp,___

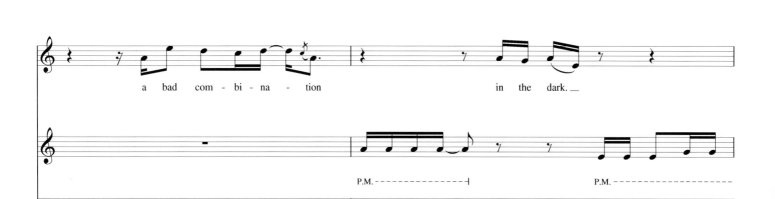

a bad com-bi-na-tion in the dark.___

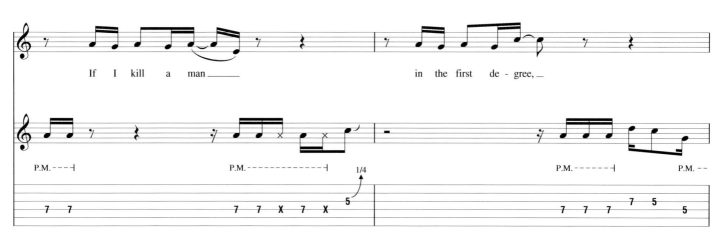

If I kill a man___ in the first de-gree,___

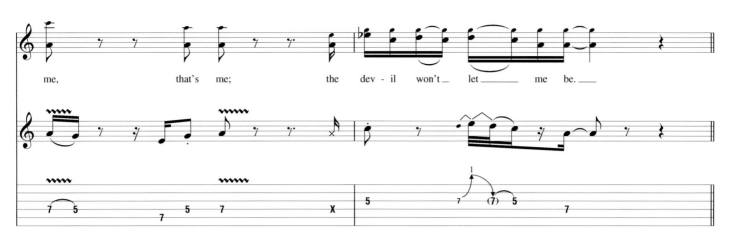

me,   that's me;   the dev - il won't __ let _____ me be. ___

Guitar Solo

Gtr. 1: w/ Riff B (4 times)

N.C.

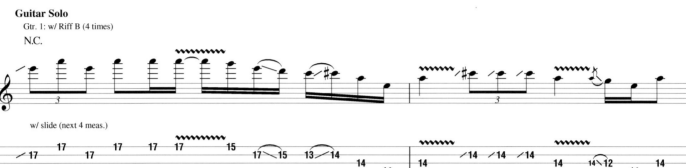

w/ slide (next 4 meas.)

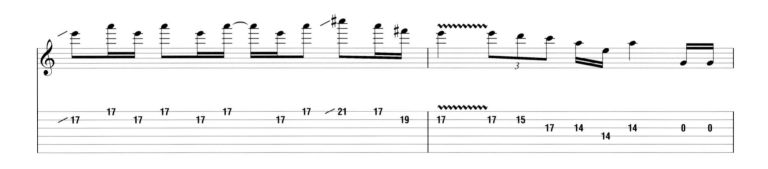

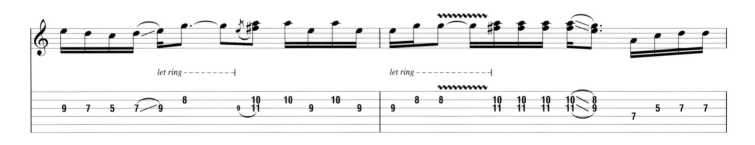

let ring - - - - - - - - -| let ring - - - - - - - - - -|

A

1/2   1/2   w/ bar

Outro
Gtr. 1: w/ Riff A (3 times)

N.C.

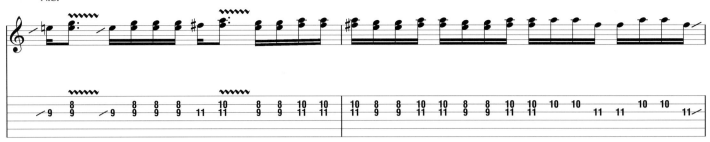

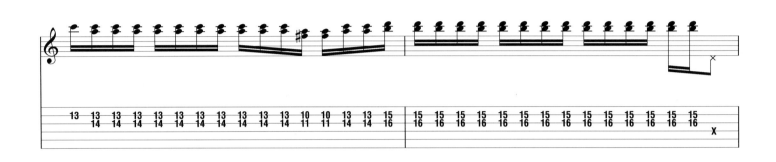

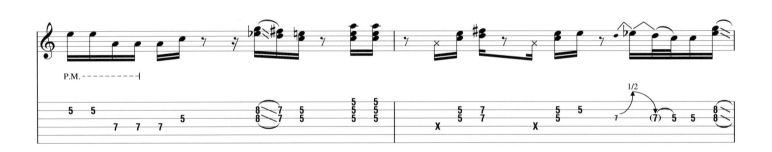

THE GO GETTER

Words and Music by
Dan Auerbach and Patrick Carney

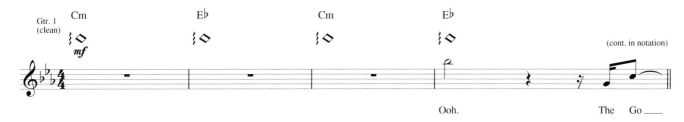

Intro
Moderately slow Rock ♩ = 78

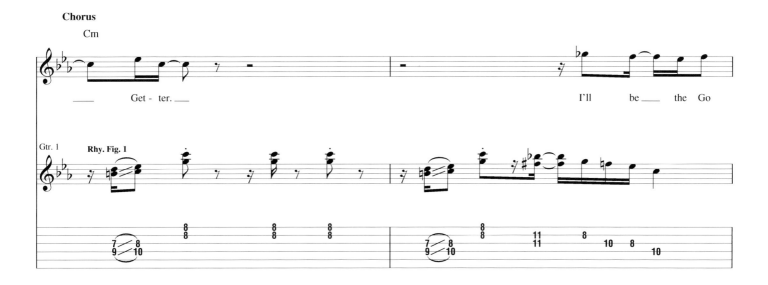

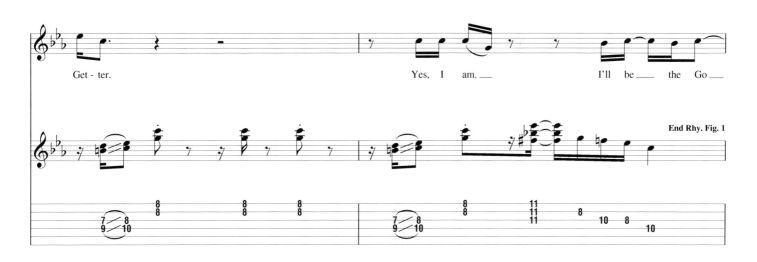

Gtr. 1: w/ Rhy. Fig. 1

____ Get - ter. ____ That's my plan. __ The Go ____ Get - ter. __

% Verse

Cm

1. Hi – fi boom box, pret - ty girls in bob - by socks. __
2. I got a ta - ble at the Rain - bow Room; I told my wife I'd be home soon.

Gtr. 1 **Rhy. Fig. 2**

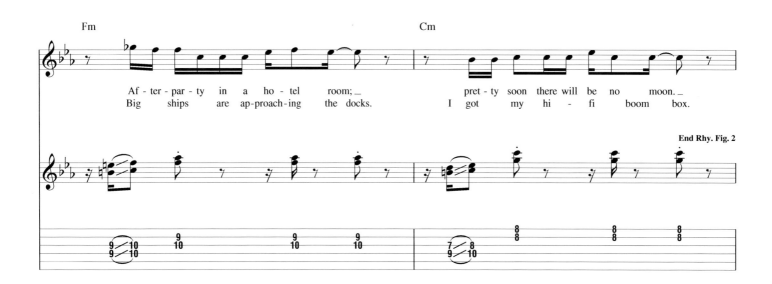

Fm   Cm

Af - ter - par - ty in a ho - tel room; __ pret - ty soon there will be no moon. __
Big ships are ap - proach - ing the docks. I got my hi – fi boom box.

End Rhy. Fig. 2

1st time, Gtr. 1: w/ Rhy. Fig. 2 (1st 3 meas.)
2nd time, Gtr. 1: w/ Rhy. Fig. 2

Stum - ble home in the pour - ing rain, __ let the wa - ter ease my __ wor - ried brain. __
Mashed po - ta - toes in cel - lo - phane. __ I see my life go - ing down the drain.

1st time, Gtr. 1: w/ Rhy. Fig. 1 (last meas.)

Fm   Cm

Some days I just can't get a - lone. __ I need a head to lean my __ shoul - ders on.
Hold me, ba - by, and don't let go. Pret - ty girls help to soft - en the blow.

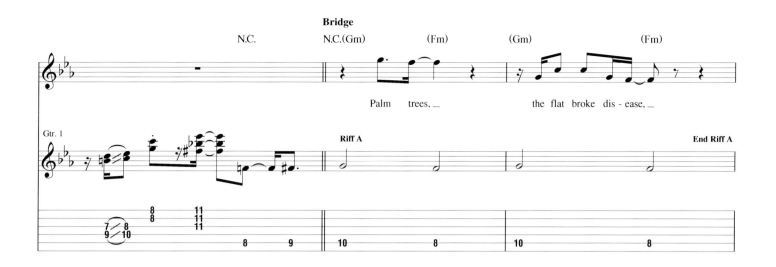

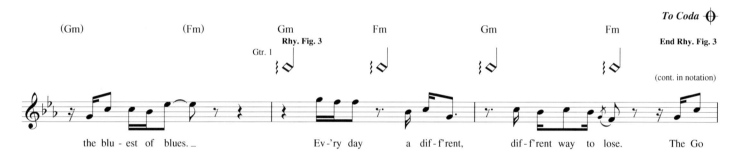

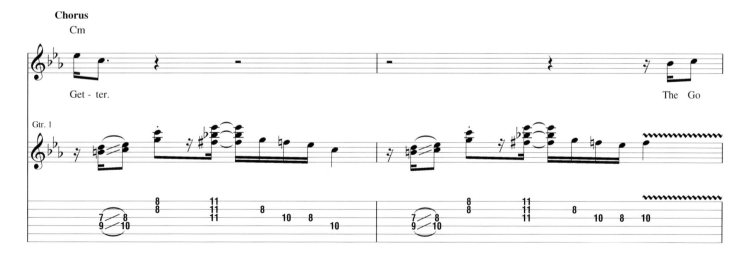

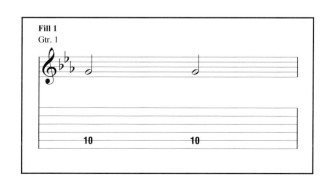

Coda

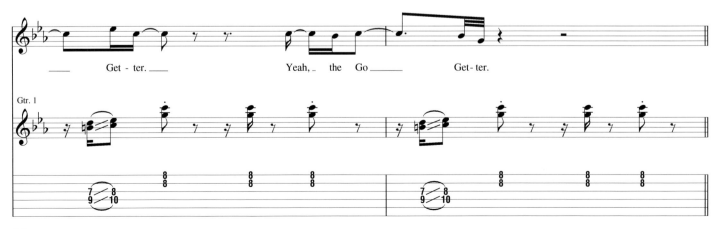

I'M NOT THE ONLY ONE

Words and Music by
Dan Auerbach and Patrick Carney

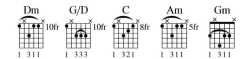

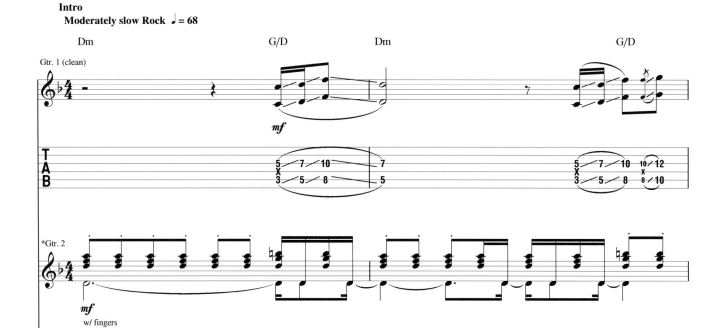

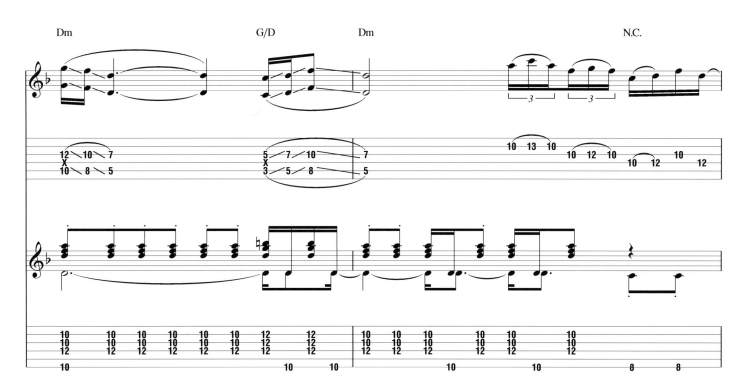

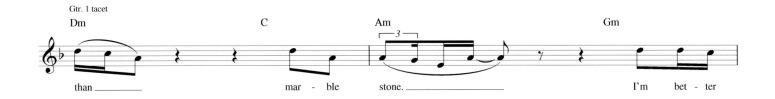

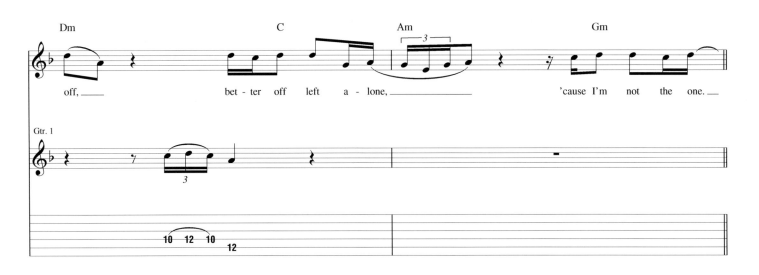

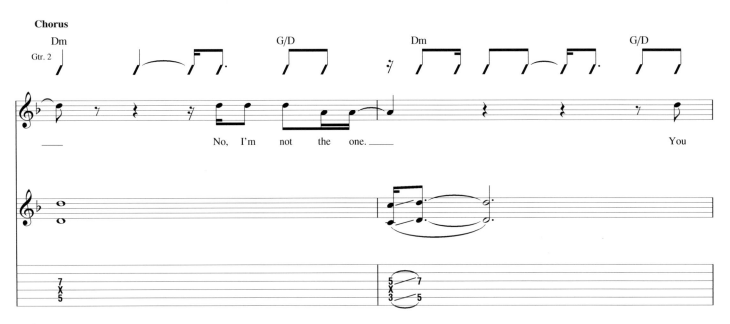

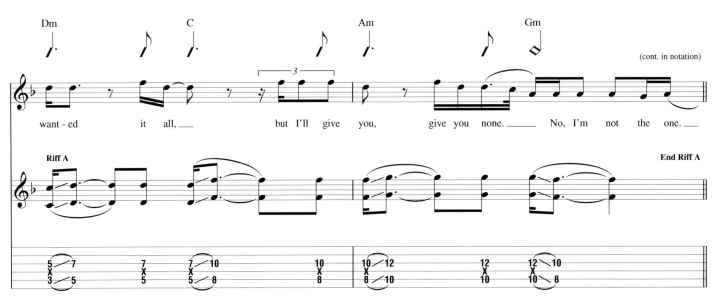

70

Interlude

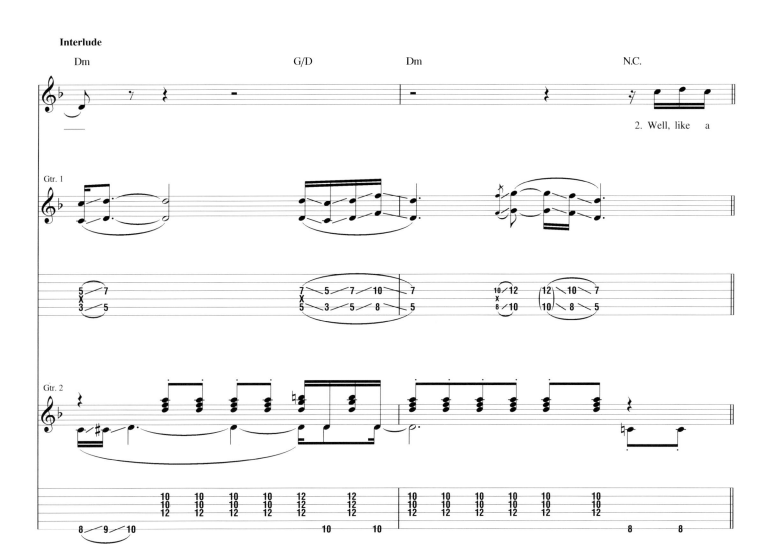

Verse

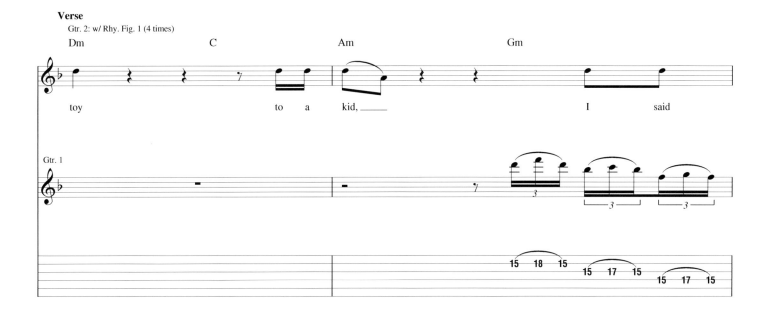

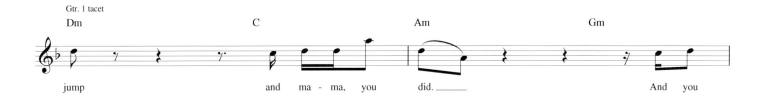

71

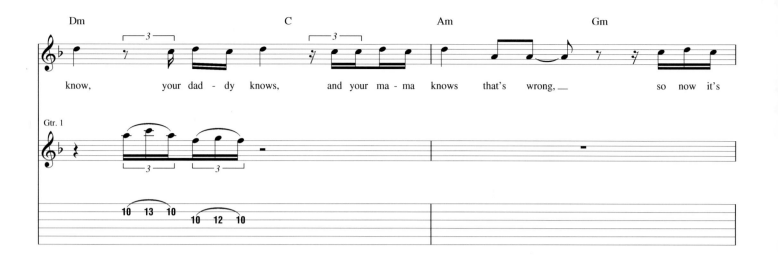

know, your dad-dy knows, and your ma-ma knows that's wrong, ___ so now it's

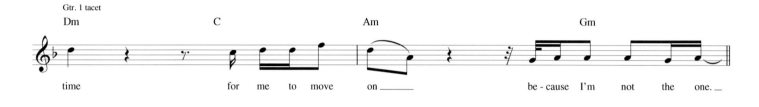

time for me to move on ___ be-cause I'm not the one. ___

Chorus

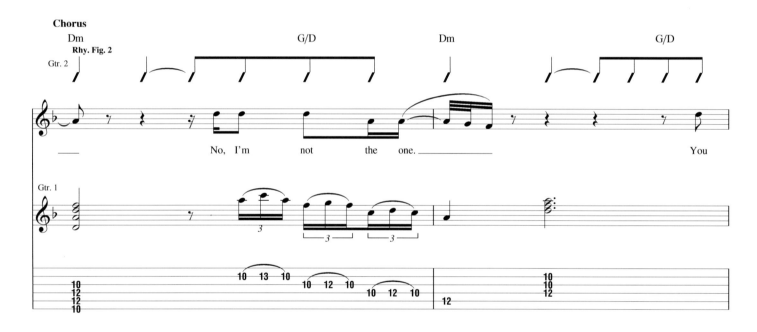

___ No, I'm not the one. ___ You

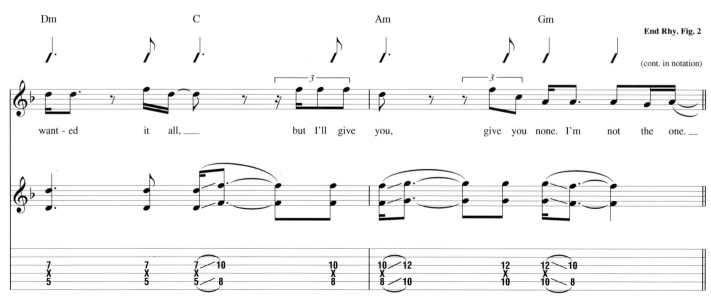

want-ed it all, ___ but I'll give you, give you none. I'm not the one. ___

Interlude

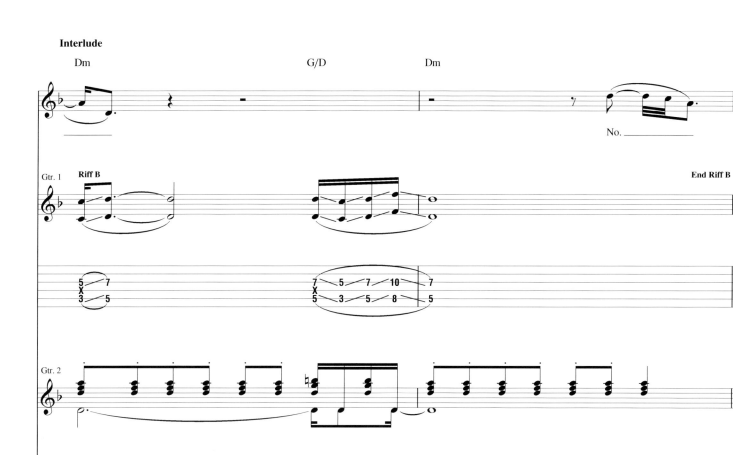

Bridge

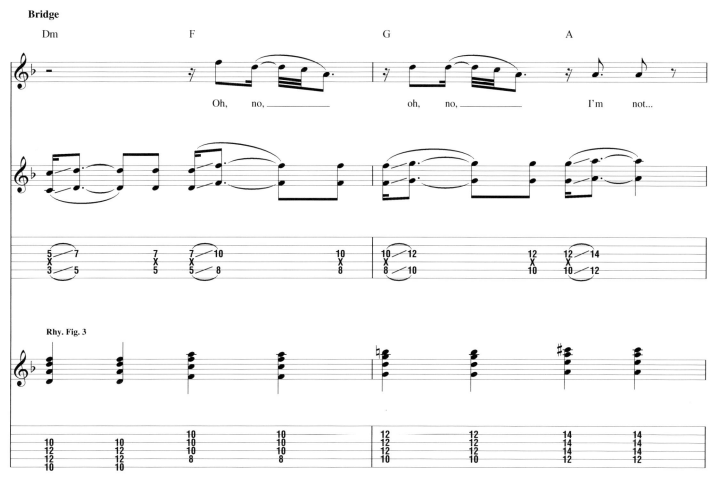

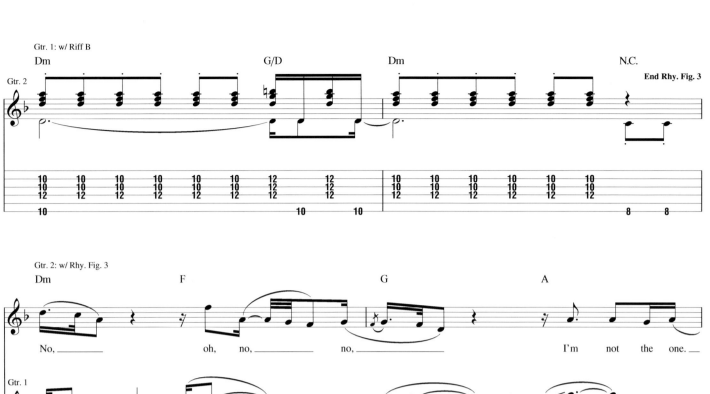

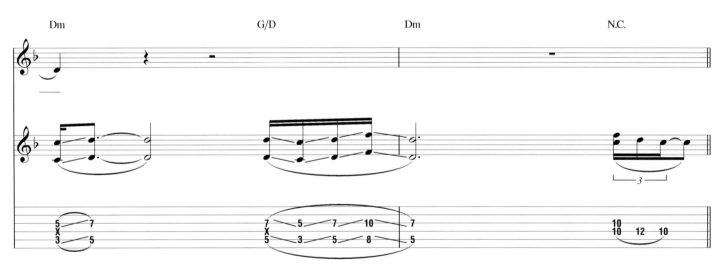

Verse

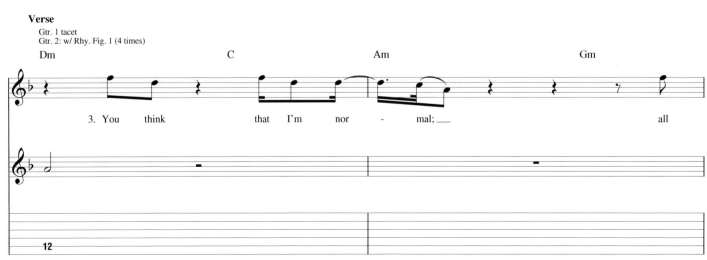

3. You think that I'm nor - mal; ___ all

74

Outro

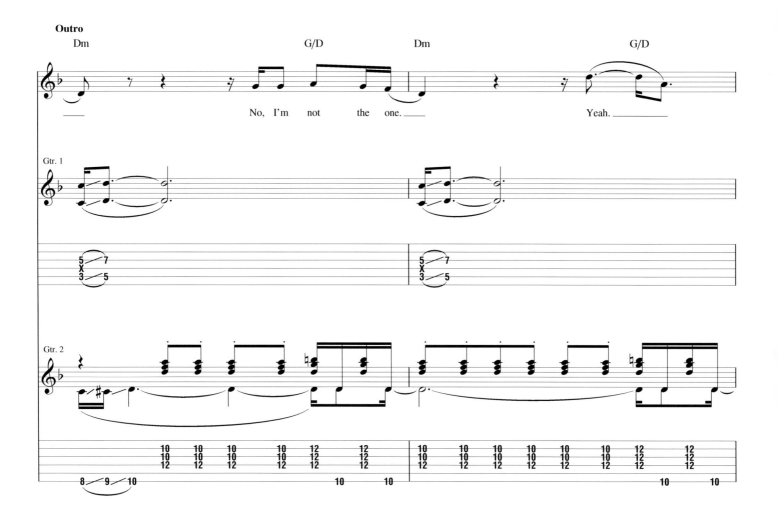

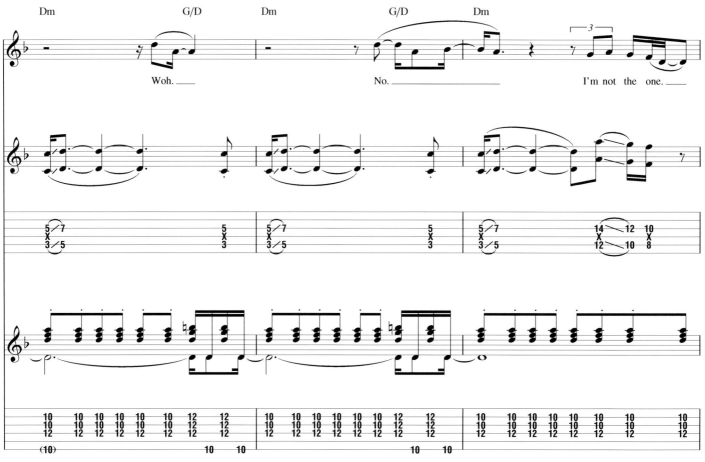

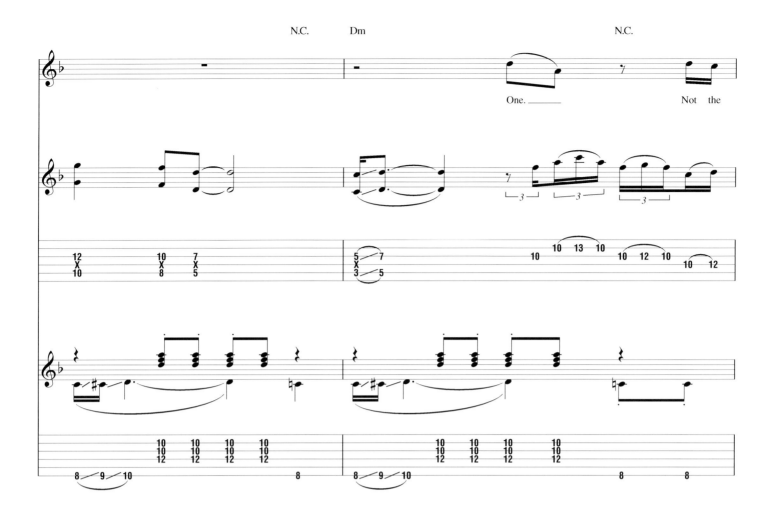

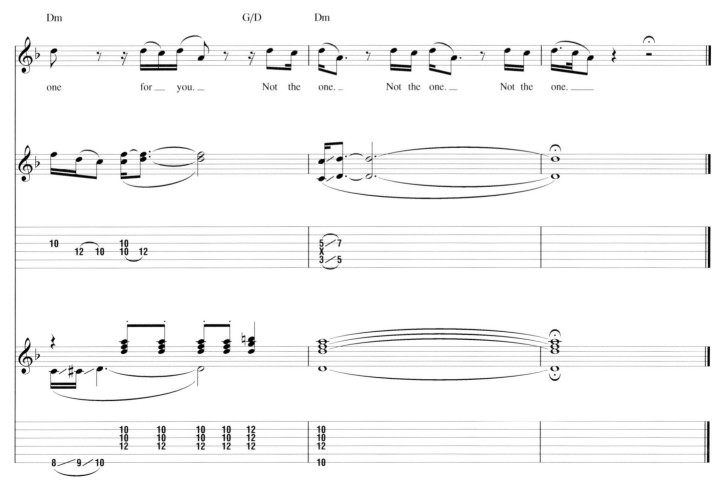

UNKNOWN BROTHER

Words and Music by
Dan Auerbach and Patrick Carney

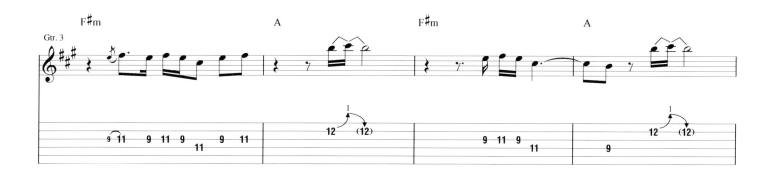

day. ___ Un - known, ___ un - known ___ broth - er, we'll

Chorus
Gtr. 1: w/ Rhy. Fig. 2 (2 times)
Gtr. 2: w/ Rhy. Fig. 1A (4 times)

walk ___ through fields ___ where chil - dren play. ___ 2. Your eyes shined ___ bright

when you ___ were a kid. ___ Your sis - ters loved you and all ___ that you did. ___

Big broth - er, big broth - er, ___ don't wor - ry a bit. ___ Your

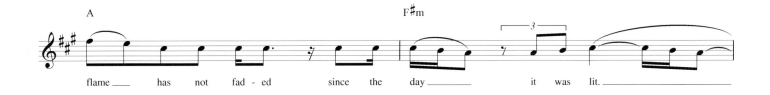

flame ___ has not fad - ed since the day ___ it was lit. ___

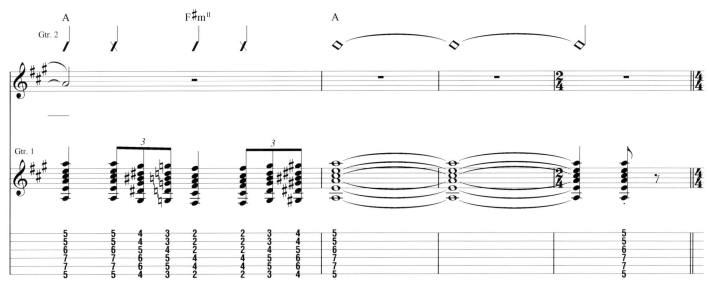

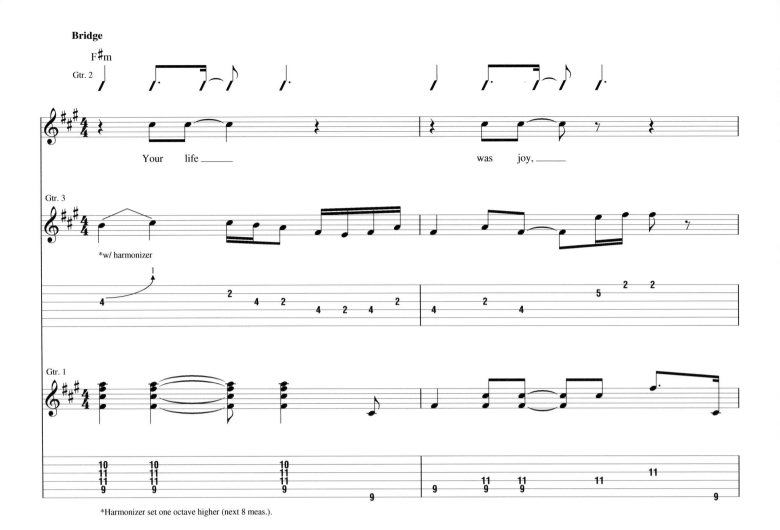

*Harmonizer set one octave higher (next 8 meas.).

82

And when the skies ___   are blue, ___

let ring - - - - - - - - - - - - - - - - - -

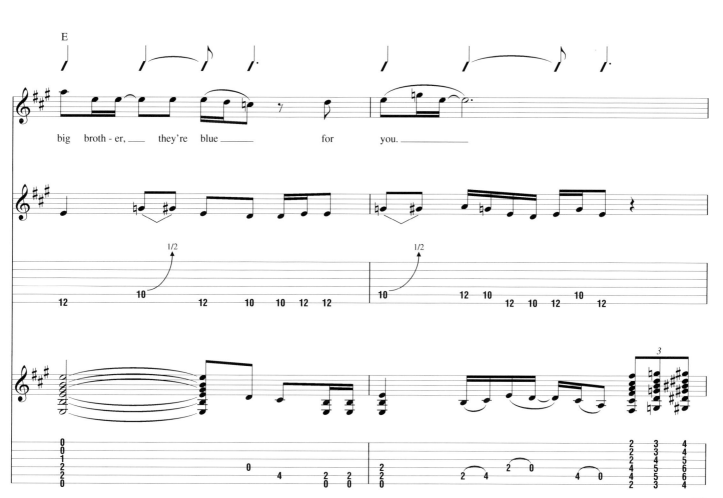

big broth - er, ___ they're blue ___   for   you. ___

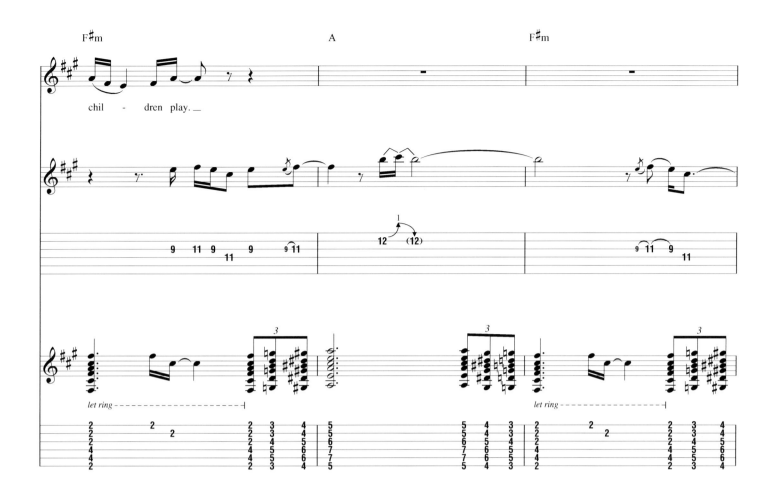

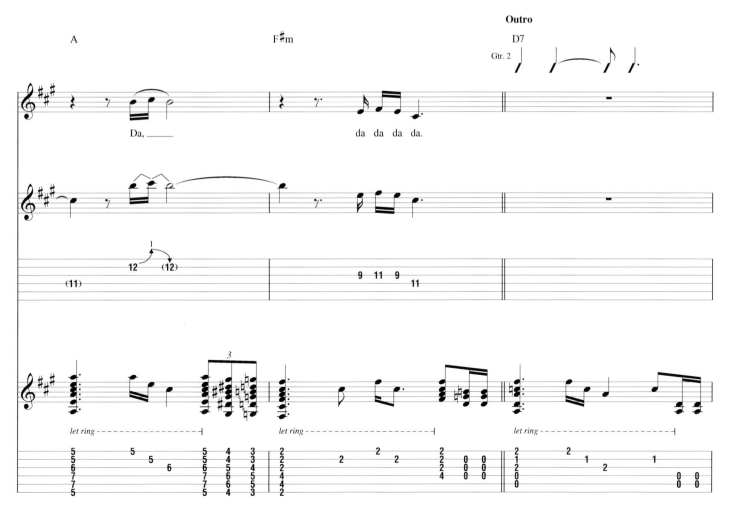

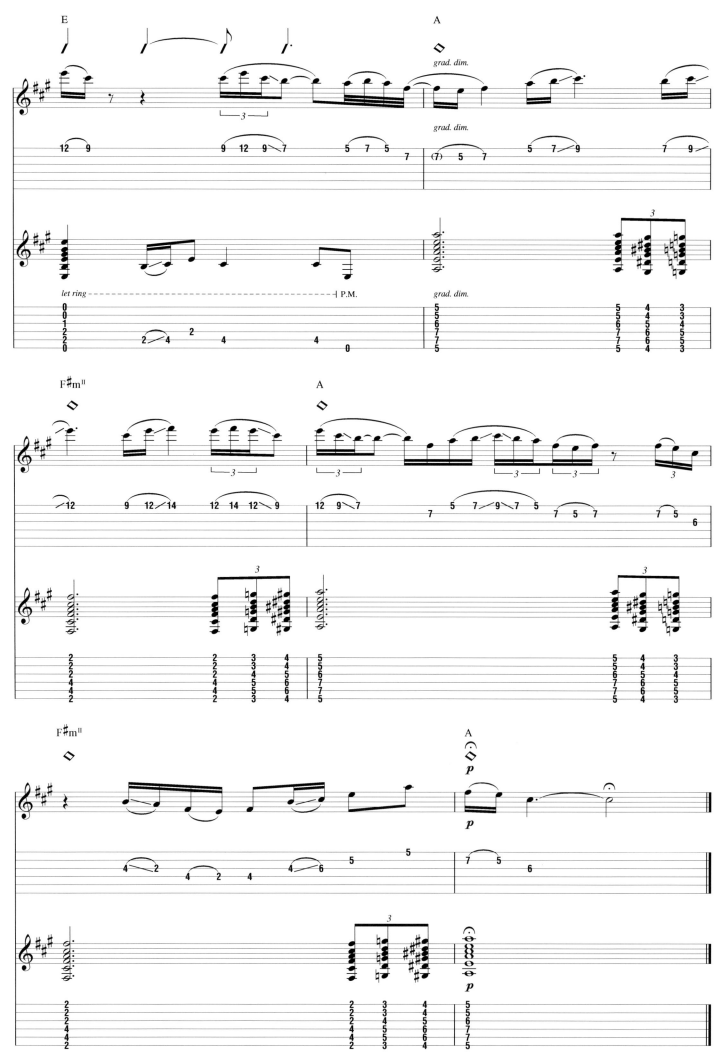

NEVER GIVE YOU UP

Words and Music by
Jerry Butler, Kenneth Gamble
and Leon Huff

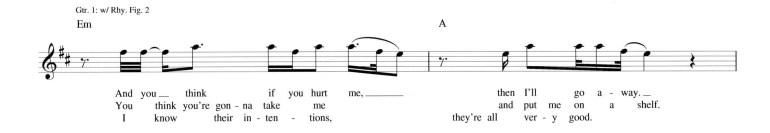

Gtr. 1: w/ Rhy. Fig. 2

And you __ think if you hurt me, _____ then I'll go a - way. __
You think you're gon - na take me and put me on a shelf.
I know their in - ten - tions, they're all ver - y good.

But I've made up my mind, ____ and you know I'm, I'm here __ to stay.
I'd rath - er die than see you with some - bod - y else.
Some of them would help me if they could. But I'm...

Chorus

Gtr. 1: w/ Rhy. Fig. 1 (2 times)

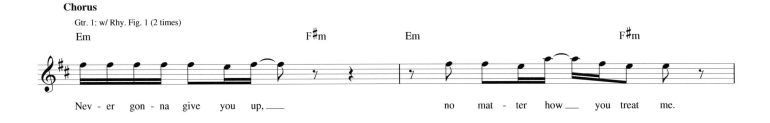

Nev - er gon - na give you up, ____ no mat - ter how __ you treat me.

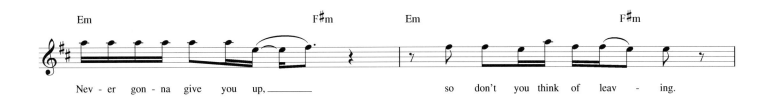

Nev - er gon - na give you up, _____ so don't you think of leav - ing.

To Coda ⊕

Gtr. 1

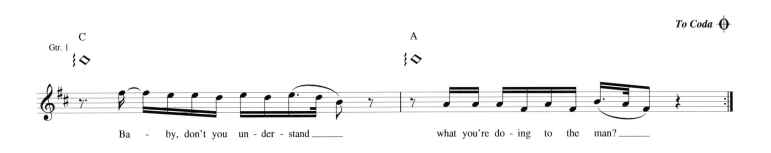

Ba - by, don't you un - der - stand ____ what you're do - ing to the man? ____

Interlude

D.S. al Coda

Gtr. 1: w/ Riff A (2 times)

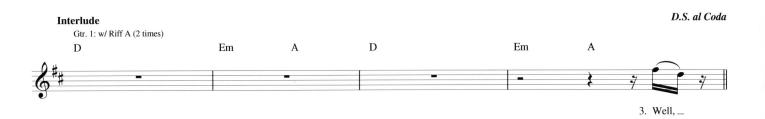

3. Well, __

88

Chorus

Gtr. 1: w/ Rhy. Fig. 1 (4 times)

Nev - er gon - na give you up, _____ no mat - ter how ___ you treat me.

Nev - er gon - na give you up, _____ so don't you think ___ of leav - ing.

Nev - er gon - na give you up, _____ no mat - ter how ___ you treat me.

Nev - er gon - na give you up, _____ so don't you think ___ of leav - ing.

Outro

Gtr. 1

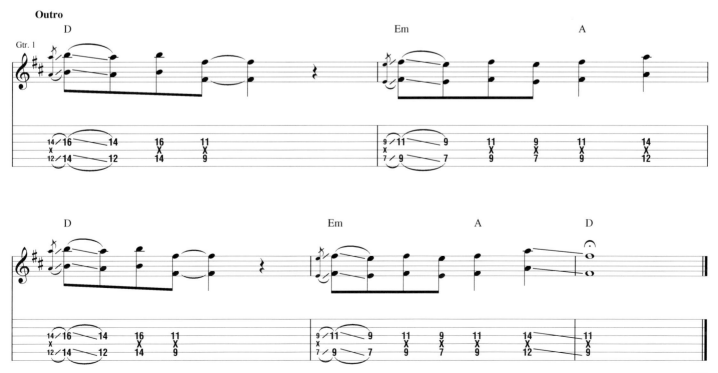

THESE DAYS

Words and Music by
Dan Auerbach and Patrick Carney

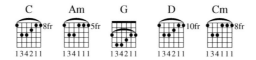

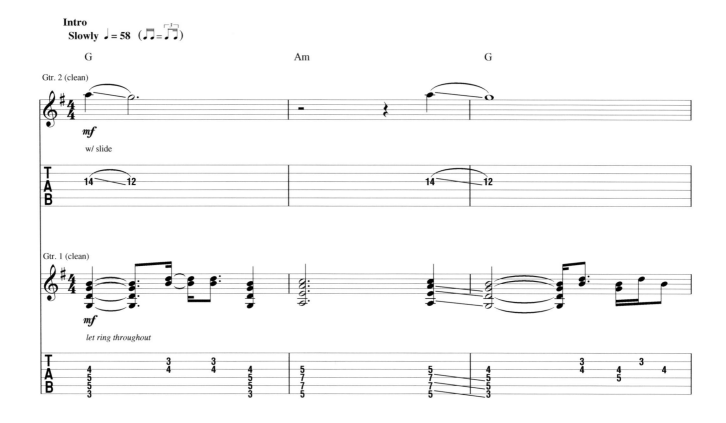

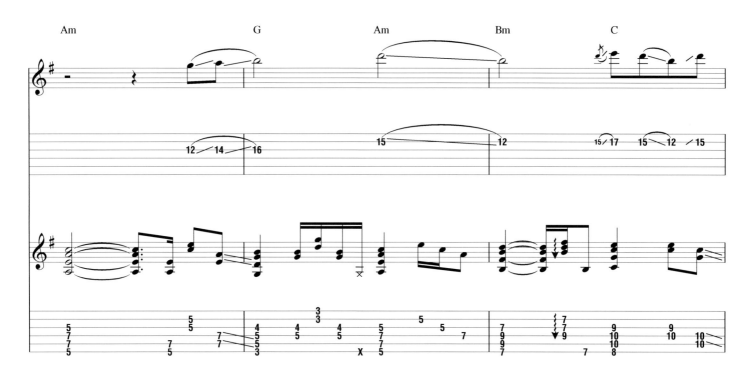

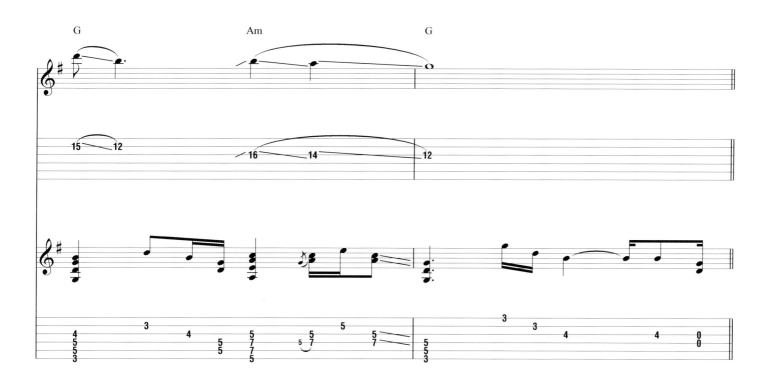

Verse

Gtr. 2 tacet

1. My hand _____ to God, I did - n't mean to. ___ Af - ter
2. The lit - tle house ___ on El - lis Drive _____

Gtr. 1

all, _____ look what we've been through.
is where I felt ___ most ___ a - live.

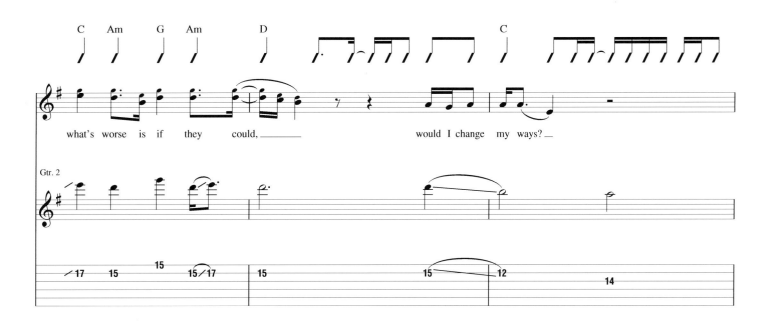

what's worse is if they could, _____ would I change my ways? __

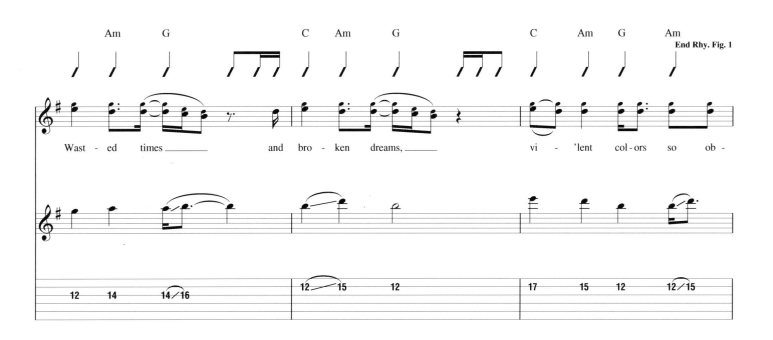

Wast - ed times _____ and bro - ken dreams, _____ vi - 'lent col - ors so ob -

End Rhy. Fig. 1

scene; ___ it's all ___ I see these days, _____ these ___ days. __

(cont. in notation)

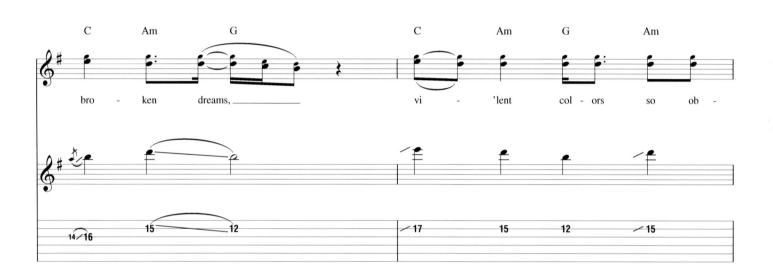

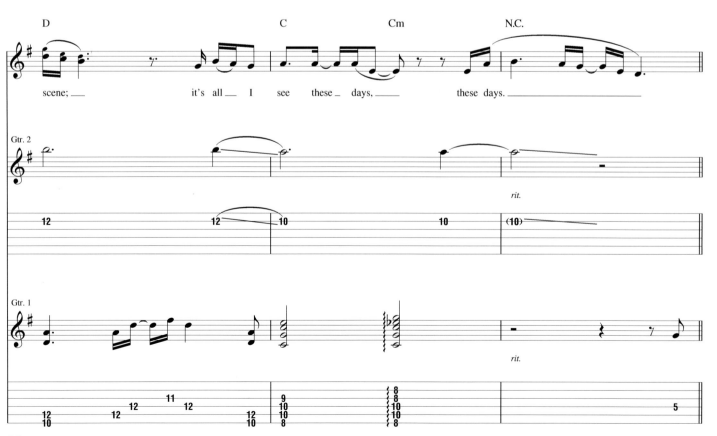

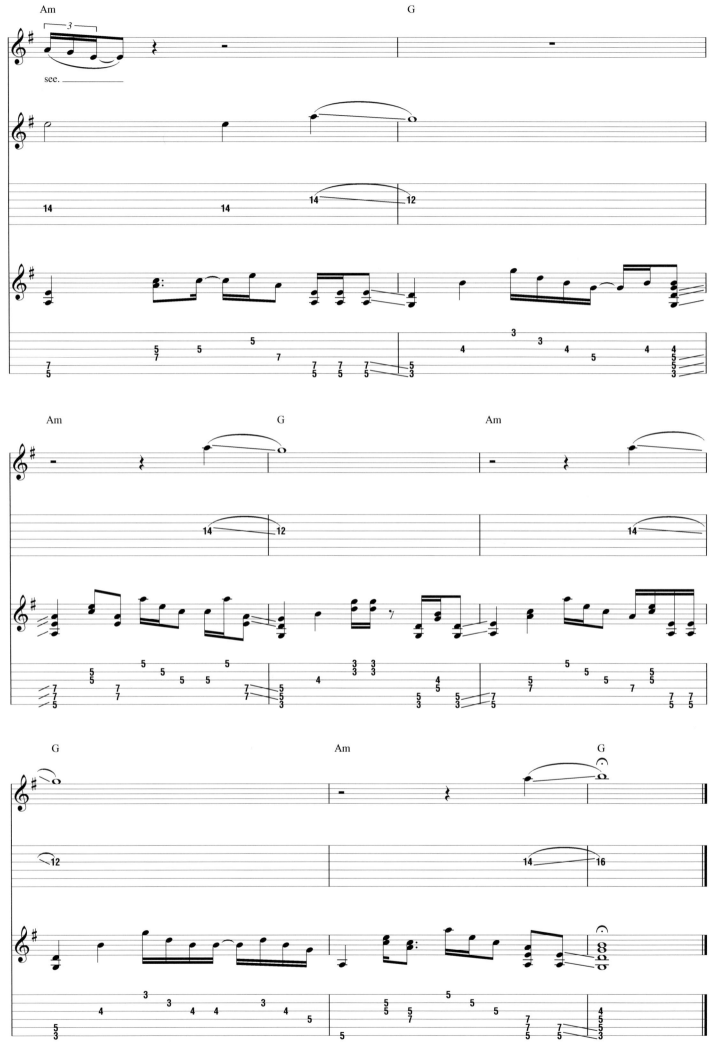

GUITAR NOTATION LEGEND

Guitar music can be notated three different ways: on a *musical staff*, in *tablature*, and in *rhythm slashes*.

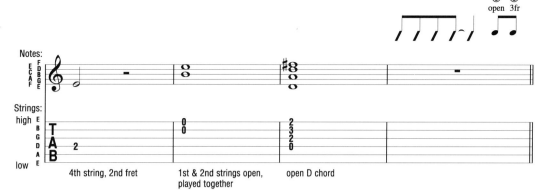

RHYTHM SLASHES are written above the staff. Strum chords in the rhythm indicated. Use the chord diagrams found at the top of the first page of the transcription for the appropriate chord voicings. Round noteheads indicate single notes.

THE MUSICAL STAFF shows pitches and rhythms and is divided by bar lines into measures. Pitches are named after the first seven letters of the alphabet.

TABLATURE graphically represents the guitar fingerboard. Each horizontal line represents a string, and each number represents a fret.

4th string, 2nd fret

1st & 2nd strings open, played together

open D chord

HALF-STEP BEND: Strike the note and bend up 1/2 step.

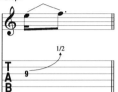

BEND AND RELEASE: Strike the note and bend up as indicated, then release back to the original note. Only the first note is struck.

HAMMER-ON: Strike the first (lower) note with one finger, then sound the higher note (on the same string) with another finger by fretting it without picking.

TRILL: Very rapidly alternate between the notes indicated by continuously hammering on and pulling off.

PICK SCRAPE: The edge of the pick is rubbed down (or up) the string, producing a scratchy sound.

TREMOLO PICKING: The note is picked as rapidly and continuously as possible.

WHOLE-STEP BEND: Strike the note and bend up one step.

PRE-BEND: Bend the note as indicated, then strike it.

PULL-OFF: Place both fingers on the notes to be sounded. Strike the first note and without picking, pull the finger off to sound the second (lower) note.

TAPPING: Hammer ("tap") the fret indicated with the pick-hand index or middle finger and pull off to the note fretted by the fret hand.

MUFFLED STRINGS: A percussive sound is produced by laying the fret hand across the string(s) without depressing, and striking them with the pick hand.

VIBRATO BAR DIVE AND RETURN: The pitch of the note or chord is dropped a specified number of steps (in rhythm), then returned to the original pitch.

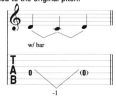

GRACE NOTE BEND: Strike the note and immediately bend up as indicated.

VIBRATO: The string is vibrated by rapidly bending and releasing the note with the fretting hand.

LEGATO SLIDE: Strike the first note and then slide the same fret-hand finger up or down to the second note. The second note is not struck.

NATURAL HARMONIC: Strike the note while the fret-hand lightly touches the string directly over the fret indicated.

PALM MUTING: The note is partially muted by the pick hand lightly touching the string(s) just before the bridge.

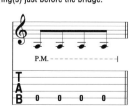

VIBRATO BAR SCOOP: Depress the bar just before striking the note, then quickly release the bar.

SLIGHT (MICROTONE) BEND: Strike the note and bend up 1/4 step.

WIDE VIBRATO: The pitch is varied to a greater degree by vibrating with the fretting hand.

SHIFT SLIDE: Same as legato slide, except the second note is struck.

PINCH HARMONIC: The note is fretted normally and a harmonic is produced by adding the edge of the thumb or the tip of the index finger of the pick hand to the normal pick attack.

RAKE: Drag the pick across the strings indicated with a single motion.

VIBRATO BAR DIP: Strike the note and then immediately drop a specified number of steps, then release back to the original pitch.

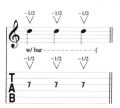

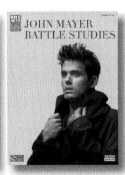
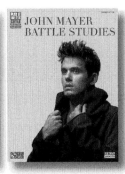